Applying Family Systems Theory to Mediation

A Practitioner's Guide

Wayne F. Regina

Dear Dr. Gilbert,

From one Bowen theory practitioner to another, I want to gift this book to you.

Most sincerely,

Wayne Regina, Psy D.

UNIVERSITY PRESS OF AMERICA,® INC.
Lanham · Boulder · New York · Toronto · Plymouth, UK

Copyright © 2011 by
University Press of America,® Inc.
4501 Forbes Boulevard
Suite 200
Lanham, Maryland 20706
UPA Acquisitions Department (301) 459-3366

Estover Road
Plymouth PL6 7PY
United Kingdom

Library of Congress Control Number: 2011927687
ISBN: 978-0-7618-5574-3 (paperback : alk. paper)
eISBN: 978-0-7618-5575-0

To my children,
Carly Bicknese Regina and Sage Bicknese Regina,
who teach me about love and laughter everyday,
and to my wife,
Janet Bicknese,
who, over the decades, has taught me more about love, life,
and work than I could have ever imagined.

In loving memory of my parents,
Antoinette Rita Regina and Eugene Regina,
who always believed that I could accomplish whatever
I set my mind to achieve.

There is nothing so practical as a good theory.

Ed Friedman

Contents

Illustrations

Preface

My professional journey in writing this book began in 1987, when I served as the program chair for United States International University's graduate programs in psychology and marriage and family therapy. We were fortunate to have a university president, Dr. William Rust, who supported efforts to bring in master practitioners to supplement the excellent work of our resident faculty. At one memorable program meeting, we brainstormed which master marriage and family therapy practitioners we were excited about bringing to campus for two-week residencies. Jim Framo, a renowned and prominent founder of the marriage and family therapy movement, was a distinguished professor in our program and a personal friend of both Murray Bowen, a pioneer in family systems theory and therapy, and one of his most well-known adherents, Edwin Friedman. Dr. Friedman's reputation as a clinician, congregational consultant, and organizational systems specialist had recently been significantly advanced by his electrifying book, *Generation to Generation*, which was published in 1985, and he was in great demand on the workshop and seminar circuit. Fortunately, with President Rust's financial commitment and our personal contact with Dr. Framo, we were able to secure Dr. Friedman for a two-week residency, which we opened to our graduate students, clinicians and clergy in the San Diego community, and faculty members at the university.

Ed's residency was nothing short of transforming for the faculty, the students, and the community. He was one of the first professionals to understand and appreciate the paradigm-changing enormity that Bowen family systems theory, also known as simply Bowen theory, had to offer. Ed had trained for years under Murray Bowen, and he applied what he learned about Bowen family systems theory to his work as a practicing rabbi and as a marriage and family therapist. His enthusiasm and towering intellect led him to expand

Bowen family systems theory to working with other human systems and organizations, including political systems, work systems, military systems, and health care systems. Others followed in expanding Bowen theory outside the parameters of treating individuals, couples, and families. For growing numbers of people, Murray Bowen's work has given them an important, systemic understanding of their personal and professional lives, and a way to consciously and intentionally advance their work in the world.

The work of Murray Bowen and Ed Friedman catalyzed me to conceptualize and apply Bowen family systems theory to my personal and professional life. Bowen theory has motivated me to find new and exciting ways of thinking about the theory and, perhaps most importantly, to applying and living the theory every day.

I am fortunate to have led a varied and diverse professional life. This is in part because I seek out new challenges to stay fresh in my professional career and in part because of my continued fascination with and appreciation for Bowen theory itself. I have been privileged to work in varied circumstances where I have had the opportunity to live the theory. Career-wise, I have served in leadership positions as a college dean, charter school director, university administrator, school board president, professor, writer, marriage and family psychologist, conciliator, supervisor, trainer, and mediator for civil, domestic, and victim-offender mediations. Each professional capacity has provided me with fresh opportunities to apply my knowledge of Bowen theory to the rich variety of human systems with which I have come in contact. Each circumstance has granted me occasions to examine my assumptions about the theory, utilize the theory in real-life situations, and "differentiate" my understanding of Bowen theory from others who use the theory for their own emotional and intellectual development. Further, I have fruitfully raised two daughters, continue in a successful thirty-plus year marriage, and remain connected with my family of origin as we age and our parents became ill and passed.

In all of my endeavors and responsibilities, I have made several important realizations about Bowen theory. First, it is a remarkably rich, nuanced, and comprehensive theory that has successfully guided me over the decades. I find it eminently pragmatic and helpful in all of my relationships. Second, "the map is not the territory," meaning that Bowen theory is a theory and translating that theory into successful life application can be gratifying as well as treacherous. While Bowen theory provides a comprehensive way of moving effectively in the world, attachment to this theory, like any theory, can actually undercut one's attempts at becoming more emotionally mature. Developing what I call passionate non-attachment is a lifelong adventure and challenge.

Third, a continual lesson, for me, is to refrain from making judgments about people's levels of emotional maturity, what Bowen calls differentiation, as well as their commitment (or non-commitment) to differentiating and becoming more responsible, productive members of their families and society. Since people naturally span levels of differentiation, judging people for being more poorly differentiated or more highly differentiated is akin to "judging" one tree for growing to a towering height and the other tree for its stunted growth. Bowen family systems theory eschews judgments in favor of observations and descriptions, and I must remain alert to this important point.

Fourth, it is easy to criticize ourselves for our faults and flaws, yet no one is perfect and imperfection is an integral part of being human. It is important that we treat ourselves with the same kind of compassion and care that we strive to treat others. In this way, we continue to promote our own differentiation process and those of others. Last, while applying Bowen theory to human systems such as mediation offers a fresh paradigm for understanding humans and human systems, it also offers us an opportunity to become more and more effective not only in our professional lives but in our personal lives as well. Removing ourselves from a short-term perspective of change that is so common in our accelerating and fast-paced society, Bowen theory, instead, offers us the opportunity to increase our emotional maturity and thus life effectiveness over decades and across situations and circumstances. This growth and development are only limited by our persistence, motivation, and determination.

In writing a book about applying Bowen family systems theory to mediation, my interest is to offer the greater mediation community the opportunity to join me in finding theoretically sound ways to understand conflict, work more effectively with disputants in resolving differences, assist people to find more successful ways to manage or even transform themselves and their conflict, and provide opportunities for us, as mediators, to increase our effectiveness, while working in highly ambiguous, often stressful, and always challenging environments. If the ultimate goal of Bowen theory and the process of differentiating is evolving ourselves and thus our species, and by so doing help transform and save the planet, and if I have helped in this process through writing a book that others find useful in their personal and professional lives, then I count that as success indeed.

Acknowledgments

There are so many people who assisted me with completing this book. Without their wisdom, I would have been hard pressed to finish. On a professional level, first, of course, I want to thank Murray Bowen for his theory, without which my life and the lives of many others would be very different. I want to also acknowledge Ed Friedman, who taught me the importance of laughter and wit; he encouraged us all to understand and apply Bowen theory to all of evolution and all of creation. His beacon of wisdom is sorely missed. Thanks, also, to Michael Kerr for *Family Evaluation*, which I fondly refer to my students as "The Bowen Bible." Dr. Kerr has worked so long and so hard to keep Dr. Bowen's work alive and expand its application through his leadership at The Bowen Center for the Study of the Family/Georgetown Family Center. I want to thank CDR Associates in Boulder, Colorado for the excellent training that they have provided to hundreds of new and experienced mediators over the years and for their important work in resolving conflict around the world.

On a personal level, I want to thank a number of people as well. First, thank you to Sally LeBoy, my co-teacher, co-writer, and co-therapist for more than ten years when I lived in San Diego. Sally is the most gifted family therapist that I have ever worked with and observed. She helped me edit large portions of this book and provided guidance when I needed it most. As a long-time friend and Bowen theory colleague, there is no other like her. Thanks, also, to K.L. Cook, author, colleague, professor at Prescott College, co-instructor, writing retreat partner, and best friend. Kenny made a great case for writing this book instead of another that I was considering and, as always, he was correct. Also, Kenny's understanding of and appreciation for Bowen theory assisted me with refining my ideas over the years, and he provided insightful and critical copy editing. I want to thank Sarah Crews, who likewise supplied useful editing and fresh eyes, especially in the final stages of the manuscript.

I want to thank Steve Pace, whose co-wrote a chapter with me entitled "The Personal Intelligences in Experiential Education: A Theory in Practice," which appeared in the 2008 book, *Theory & Practice of Experiential Education*. I used that chapter as a basis for chapter 12, "Training and Supervising Mediators Using Bowen Theory."

I also want to thank my retreat buddy and good friend Tim Crews for years of lively conversation around a variety of topics, Prescott College for providing me with the freedom to explore my passion and teach numerous classes centered around applications of Bowen family systems theory, and Kathy McCormick and Heather Seets from the Yavapai County Superior Court of Arizona for providing abundant opportunities to conduct mediations and marital conciliations, and to train and supervise the gifted mediators in their excellent program.

Finally, I want to thank my family for supporting me and believing in me, including my parents Eugene Regina and Antoinette Regina, who always provided love and encouragement for my dreams; my siblings, Gary, Ronald, and Debra Regina, my in-laws, Sussie Regina and Bart Broome, and my nephew, Jesse Regina, for their dedication to and love for our extended family; my daughters, Carly and Sage Regina, for their love, humor, intelligence, and sensitivity and for growing up to become such remarkable young women; and, finally, to my wife of over thirty years, Janet Bicknese, for providing so much that it is hard to put in words. Janet edited early versions of the manuscript, and over the years she has become my favorite co-mediator. As a teacher, musician, co-mediator, co-writer, parent, and life partner, more than anyone else, Janet has helped me to discover the true meaning of differentiation.

Part I

BOWEN FAMILY SYSTEMS THEORY

Chapter One

Why Bowen Family Systems Theory?

Many excellent books and articles have been written about mediation. By and large, these publications addressed the historical roots of conflict and conflict resolution, articulated the mediation process and the stages of mediation, and described techniques used by effective mediators (Adler, 1984; Moore, 1983). The specific types of mediation and mediation processes reviewed include peer mediation, victim-offender mediation and dialogue, domestic mediation, environmental mediation, business-labor mediations, community mediation, and transformative mediation, to name a few. Many writers approach mediation from a practical, technical, and atheoretical perspective, choosing to focus on the mechanics of the mediation process or on a particular stage or technique. While some authors reference theories of conflict and conflict resolution in advocating for alternative dispute resolution processes like mediation, attempts to ground mediation in a comprehensive theoretical system are rare (MacFarlane & Mayer, 2005; Raines, Hedeen, & Barton, 2010; Regina, 2000). The field of mediation clearly lacks a unifying theoretical foundation. In this book, I present a comprehensive theoretical model, based on the work of Murray Bowen, a pioneer in family systems theory, to support the growing interest in and development of the field of mediation. Murray Bowen's family systems theory, often referred to as Bowen theory or Bowen family systems theory, offers an all-inclusive theoretical model that describes important aspects of family and human functioning through a systemic lens, one that views human behavior through an intricate web of emotional processes linked to that of all living systems (Bowen, 1971, 2002).

While Bowen theory was initially developed as an alternative, comprehensive, and systemic understanding of families, its unique perspective on humans and human behavior as a function of both interpersonal and intrapersonal forces has led to the theory's application and expansion beyond the family to other complex, human systems, including business (Miller, 2002; Wiseman, 1996), leadership (Friedman, 1996, 2007; Gilmore, 1982), education (Cook & Regina, 2006; Dillow, 1996; Regina & Pace, 2007), health care (Sobel, 1982; Hilbert, 1996), and congregations (Friedman, 1985; Steinke, 2006).

This book applies Bowen theory to another important area of human in-teractions, namely, conflict resolution through mediation. As a practicing mediator and professor of peace studies and psychology, I offer an in-depth, theoretical understanding of mediation techniques, the systemic relationship between disputants, the importance of the mediator's emotional maturity and the co-mediator relationship, the effect of multiple parties (including attorneys and stakeholder groups) on the mediation process, and the overall importance of theory in practice.

I propose this comprehensive theoretical understanding of mediation for two reasons. First, mediation articles, books, and training programs often present mediation simply as a technical set of skills to be mastered, a process of varying degrees of formality or informality through which conflict can be managed and agreements can be written. In effect, many assume the media-tors and disputants can merely follow a delineated process in order to suc-ceed. Nothing could be further from the truth. While a clearly articulated and defined process *is* an important component for success, understanding human nature and human behavior through a systemic lens is crucial for maximizing success in mediation. Bowen theory offers a profound way to conceptualize both the process and the content of the mediation experience. As such, I write this book in hopes that it will help ground the profession of mediation as a rigorous academic discipline and as a way to integrate theory, research, and practice in mediation. Secondly, and perhaps more pragmatically, I write this book to provide a guide for the mediation practitioner, one that will help the mediator successfully navigate the often-intense, emotional minefield of me-diation. As Ed Friedman (1991), a protégé and important colleague of Murray Bowen, was often fond of saying when referring to Bowen theory, "There is nothing so practical as a good theory."

A comprehensive theory about mediation can provide a sensible and pragmatic roadmap to clarify what you are seeing and where you want to go as a mediator. And while the map is not the territory, the theory offers a pathway to understand, emotionally and intellectually, where you are and where you want to travel by more clearly defining the journey ahead of time. This map better prepares us, as mediators, to manage the multiple variables, unforeseen circumstances, obstacles along the way, and opportunities for positive change when they appear. Perhaps the most significant benefit of having a solid grounding in theory is that, as mediators, we can better focus on understanding mediation as a systems phenomenon and our responsibility to managing ourselves and the process of mediation. This grounding allows us, in turn, to remain clearheaded and not get lost in the emotional logic and emotional reactivity generated and amplified by highly charged people in decidedly anxious situations associated with heated negotiations and intense disagreements. If, as mediators, we can develop and hold a centered—or, as Bowen puts it, a more "differentiated"—presence, that is, not easily reacting to the reactivity of others, and understand what we are seeing though the lens of Bowen theory, we are more likely to facilitate a successful resolution of conflict. Even if the mediation does not produce an agreement, as mediators, we can avoid "losing our heads" and undercutting the very mediation process that we are trying to facilitate.

In this book, I will first describe the essential Bowen theory concepts relevant to mediation. I will articulate the theory's core components and demonstrate their application to the mediation process. Next, I will review the stages of mediation and define them through the theory. I will re-conceptualize the traditional six-stage, North American mediation model as something more than a set of "do's and don'ts," but rather, as a model best understood and implemented through the theory itself. I will describe common errors in mediation and how an understanding of Bowen theory can minimize them.

As with any organizational system, the emotional functioning of the system's leadership is the single most important variable for effective functioning of the system and, in mediation, the mediator is the leader. Thus, I will describe the overriding importance of the mediator's level of emotional maturity to mediation outcome. I will then discuss critical theoretical concerns such as emotional triangles, triangulation, and de-triangulation as they are relevant to mediation. Understanding emotional triangles and triangulation is essential for learning to "think systems" and for not getting snared by the anxiety of disputants, their attorneys, and their stakeholder groups.

I will describe the relationship between attachment and differentiation and how attachment to outcome and over-functioning undercuts the mediation process and the disputants' capacity to work effectively for their own solutions. I will present important information on current brain research—including hyper-arousal, the fight-flight mechanism, and emotional reactivity—and how these evolutionary variables can affect mediation and disputant reactions. I will offer suggestions for both understanding and monitoring disputant fight-flight reactions; for developing increased capacity to manage one's own reactivity and those of disputants, their attorneys, and their stakeholders; and how the emotional state of the mediators can effect positive change. I will reformat important mediation techniques such as caucusing, brainstorming, and shuttle mediation, and mediation concepts including the role of neutrality, attachment, and balance through the lens of the Bowen theory. I will discuss diversity distinctions and how they are conceptualized through Bowen theory. Finally, using Bowen theory as a guide, I will analyze a variety of specific mediation and alternative dispute resolution processes, including domestic mediations and conciliations, as well as present a model for training mediators.

It is my hope that the reader will find this book theoretically clear and useful, and effective for making the shift into systems thinking. By understanding human nature, human behavior, and human relationships more fully, we may each achieve a higher level of self-responsibility and personal effectiveness as individuals and in our roles as mediators. With this increased capacity, we can advance the mediation profession and enhance the entire mediation process to better achieve our goal of helping disputants more peacefully resolve their differences.

The next chapter provides an overview of the essential Bowen theory concepts relevant to mediation.

Chapter Two

Understanding Bowen Family Systems Theory

This book cannot do justice to the complexity and extensiveness of Bowen family systems theory. As a theoretical system, Bowen theory is over fifty years old. It is elaborate, elegant, complex, and simple all at once. Other writers have detailed a comprehensive understanding and articulation of Bowen theory. Excellent references include Murray Bowen (2002) himself, Edwin Friedman (1991), Daniel Papero (1990), Michael Kerr (1981), and Michael Kerr and Murray Bowen (1988). Bowen originally conceptualized a theory to understand human and family functioning and to treat families in clinical settings. While the bulk of Bowen theory remains focused on clinical applications, including working with individuals, couples, and families, almost from the very beginning, people understood the value of applying the theory to a variety of disciplines and human endeavors. As such, Bowen theory has been applied to organizations and leadership (Ferrera, 1996; Friedman, 1996, 2007; Gilbert, 1996; McCullough, 1996; Bowen, 2002), education (Dillow, 1996), congregations (Friedman, 1985, Steinke, 2006), nonhuman systems (Ferrera, 1996), and particular aspects of family systems and family functioning (Kerr and Bowen, 1988; Regina and LeBoy, 1991; Schnarch, 1997; Carter and McGoldrick, 2005). The same principles that apply to other human systems make Bowen theory a natural theoretical fit for mediation. Rather than recreate the work of these seminal writers, theoreticians, clinicians, and practitioners, I will instead discuss the central concepts relevant to mediation and encourage the reader to explore this far-reaching theory in more detail through the references listed.

One of the challenges in presenting an overview of Bowen theory is that the concepts are highly interdependent and interrelated. As such, it is difficult to explain one concept without using other concepts that have not yet been fully articulated. Nonetheless, this overview is an attempt to explain the

concepts within the context of mediation. When related concepts are introduced early on, I request the reader's patience, as the interrelationship of the
concepts will eventually be made clear.

A BRIEF HISTORY OF BOWEN THEORY

In the 1950s and 1960s, psychodynamic psychologies based on the work
of Sigmund Freud (1959) and his associates, behaviorism centered on the
theories of B.F. Skinner's (1972), and the so-called "third force" humanistic
perspectives of Carl Rogers (1951), Abraham Maslow (1968), Victor Frankl
(1959) and their associates dominated psychology, psychiatry, and models
of human behavior. All three of these theoretical and clinical branches as-
sumed the primacy of the individual in understanding human behavior and
treating psychological disorders. It was in this environment in the 1950s that
Murray Bowen (1966; 1971) began his professional career as a psychiatrist,
except that he, like other radical psychiatrists and psychologists of the time,
began rejecting the dogma of theory and treatment based solely on individual
models. These pioneers began incorporating new approaches to treatment and
formulating new theories for health and pathology. Out of this creative firma-
ment, family systems theories were born in their many manifestations. James
Framo (1992: 2003) and Henry Dicks (1953) developed object relations family theory and therapy. Gregory Bateson, Don Jackson, Jay Haley, and John
Weakland (1956), Virginia Satir (1983), and others created communications-
based family theory and therapy (Wynne, Ryckoff, Day, and Hirsch, 1958).
Carl Whittaker and Thomas Malone (1953) founded symbolic-experiential
family theory and therapy. Jay Haley (1963) was instrumental in formulating strategic family theory and therapy. These schools of family therapy
represent samplings of the important work occurring during this pivotal time.
Rather than simply focusing on family therapy techniques and methods,
Murray Bowen (1966) boldly articulated a comprehensive theory of human
functioning based on observations of families and other natural systems (Kerr
and Bowen, 1988).

Murray Bowen was a medical doctor who specialized in psychiatry. He
lived from 1913 to 1990. While trained in traditional psychoanalytical approaches, Bowen also studied with Harry Stack Sullivan, a psychiatrist interested in the more social aspects of psychiatry, rather than simply the internal,
intrapsychic factors of human existence associated with psychoanalytic psychiatry. Sullivan's influence and Bowen's innate curiosity about the natural
world led him to look at the connections between people and the natural
world. For Bowen the scientist, speculation about internal forces of the hu-

man mind lacked the kind of rigor and scrutiny that observation offered. As such, Murray Bowen began developing a theory of family functioning that was more "objective"; that is, his approach was rooted in current and multi-generational observations of human and family interactions and did not infer internal processes. With a focus on observable systems, Bowen's developing theory was thus profoundly different from Freud's prevailing psychoanalytical model that relied on conjecture and supposition.

BOWEN THEORY CONCEPTS RELEVANT TO MEDIATION

Individuality and Togetherness Life Forces

Bowen's emerging theory was also fundamentally different from Freud's theory in a second way: Bowen analyzed the intimate interrelationship with and connection between the human and non-human world. He keenly observed nature and natural processes. His family systems theory was predicated on his observations that the same fundamental forces that governed all life, if not all creation, governed the human species. Bowen called these forces *individuality* and *togetherness* (Kerr and Bowen, 1988). He described individuality as a universal, biological life force that propels organisms toward separateness, uniqueness, and distinctiveness. He saw all life forms expressing this drive toward becoming distinct entities. Bowen explained togetherness as the complementary, universal, biological life force that propels organisms toward relationship, attachment, and connectedness. For Bowen, it was the relationship between these dialectic life forces that determined an organism's level of *differentiation*, that is, its capacity to function as a distinctly separate organism, while remaining in intimate connection with others and its environment. Bowen viewed humans as simply one example of how these fundamental forces expressed themselves in nature.

As such, Bowen considered humans as an extension of nature rather than as separate from the natural world. In this way, Bowen theory is a ecological model that seeks to understand humans as part of a natural, emotional ecosystem, whereas Freud's theory emphasized our uniqueness as a species, with our development and functioning governed by internal processes that regard humans as more distinctive and separate from nature.

The Emotional System

In contrast to Freud's psychoanalytic theory and other established individual-based models of human development and functioning dominant at the time,

Bowen theory emphasized natural processes and life forces that connect humans to evolutionary history. In fact, Bowen's evolutionary perspective led him to theorize that most human behavior was not merely socially-conditioned or intra-psychically generated but automatic behavior rooted in billions of years of evolutionary development. In essence, Bowen believed that most of our behavior and ascribed motivation is not so much a factor of cognitive thinking or expression of feelings but, rather, a function of habitual processes that are expressed beyond conscious choice or control. He called this depth of automatic functioning and reactivity the *emotional system* and he distinguished this system from the feeling system and the thinking or intellectual system (Kerr and Bowen, 1988). Like the moth drawn to the flame, the ant storing food for the colony, the fish swimming in tight school formations, or the woman yelling at the driver who cut her off, emotional functioning through the emotional system represent behavior that is automatic and reactive.

Bowen postulated that humans are more similar to than different from other forms of life. Like lesser developed life forms, Bowen said that much of our behavior is automatic, based on all that was "written" before in nature. This emotional system is, in part, based in our primitive, "reptilian" brain, but is not simply an expression of brain functioning. Friedman (1991) suggests that the emotional system is more properly conceptualized as operating at a cellular level, leading to behavior that is reflexive or reactive. Bowen theory contends that humans share this automatic reactivity with all living creatures (Kerr and Bowen, 1988). While humans might ascribe these behaviors to various cognitive or feeling-based motivations, Bowen believed that these assignments are merely "surface" understandings and explanations of "deeper" processes. From this perspective, then, most human behavior, including interactions with others, is an expression that goes beyond the human. It connects humanity with all biotic life.

Bowen conceptualized the emotional system as a complex amalgamation of nature *and* nurture, with influences that include genes and their expression; current environmental factors such as life experiences and circumstances; multigenerational patterns; family functioning and family process; sibling position; and a host of additional and significant social, environmental, and emotional factors. This expression in the emotional system, particularly in highly stressful situations and environments, results in emotional reactivity that has clear roots in survival mechanisms.

For example: two drivers, Sam and Matthew, have an altercation on the road. This leads to a variety of reflexive posturing reactions (yelling and screaming, exchanging obscene hand gestures, etc.). A multitude of factors in his emotional system predisposes Sam to escalate the conflict and follow Matthew. These factors include a genetic predisposition to violence, a family history of abuse or conflict, as well as current issues such as a recent loss of a job and marital strife. Sam is more likely to become hyper-aroused as he experiences threat and his fight-flight reaction becomes activated. As a result, Sam follows Matthew looking for a fight. Sam's accumulated life experience does not include taking personal responsibility for his actions, and others view him as impulsive and immature. That is, Sam lacks the capacity for effective self-reflection and self-regulation in moderately to highly stressful situations, and consequently his behavior is more automatic and "mindless." After the incident is over, Sam might rationalize his behavior as wanting to "teach the other guy a lesson" or feeling angry that the driver cut him off at a traffic light. These justifications, though, are partial and inadequate. More accurately, Sam's behavior is an emotional reaction to a perceived threat. Sam's capacity to manage his reaction is hampered by the variety of emotional factors previously listed, and his level of emotional maturity or differentiation is fairly low. He lacks the capacity to stop his actions from escalating after the initial incident.

Matthew, by contrast, initially reacts automatically as well. His threat activation system is also engaged, and he, too, yells, screams, and displays a variety of obscene gestures. While initially hyper-aroused, Matthew's accumulated life experience includes taking more personal responsibility for his actions. He has a greater capacity for both self-reflection and self-regulation and, as a result, when Sam starts following him, he tries to regain his composure and think his way out of the escalation. Matthew pulls over to the side of the road, exits his car in a non-threatening way with his hands in clear view, demonstrating a gesture of conciliation, approaches Sam, and apologizes for his actions at the intersection and for escalating the conflict. Matthew's calm demeanor and self-focused, personal responsibility help calm Sam, and the incident rapidly de-escalates. Matthew's level of emotional maturity or differentiation is clearly much higher than that of Sam, and his capacity to remain relatively calm—that is, to self-regulate his behavior, accept personal responsibility, and make a positive connection with Sam—soothes the two-person system and resolves the conflict. Matthew demonstrates a higher capacity for autonomous behavior rather than simply reacting automatically throughout the crisis.

While emphasizing our connectedness to all life and natural evolutionary processes, Bowen did not discount what makes humans unique. In fact, Bowen understood that humans have unique abilities to go beyond our predetermined and automatic behavioral patterns and respond more thoughtfully and independently. Bowen discussed our uniqueness as a species through the evolution of a highly developed feeling system (as contrasted with the evolutionarily older emotional system), as well as a decidedly advanced thinking or intellectual system (Kerr and Bowen, 1988). Bowen said that it was the intellectual system, and its most evolutionarily advanced features in the prefrontal lobe, where higher order thinking takes place (planning, foresight, and so forth), that allows us to respond differently from our animal cousins. That is, Bowen recognized that the human brain had developed a remarkable capacity for reflection, clear thinking, and understanding consequences of various personal choices, thereby allowing more reflective and mindful responses rather than always reacting mindlessly. While articulating a set of central concepts that are based on our connection to natural systems and processes, Bowen also demonstrated how, with a concerted effort over time, humans are capable of modifying some of our automatic expressions in order to respond more consciously and intentionally. In the above example, Matthew demonstrated this possibility of more self-determined behavior.

One of the hallmarks of Bowen theory is the notion that humans are social animals who have developed the capacity to move beyond their systems "programming" and respond thoughtfully rather than instinctively (Friedman, 1991). While humans have this capacity for independent response, Bowen said that in stressful and thus emotional times, it must be carefully cultivated or else we are likely to react reflexively rather than respond creatively, with mindfulness. He defined this capacity for greater self-determination as *differentiation*.

In mediation, disputants' differentiation levels, that is, their capacity to think clearly and thoughtfully or react more automatically and defensively, is a significant factor regarding success. But perhaps not so obviously, the mediator's differentiation level, or ability to self-soothe and self-regulate, is an even more important variable in mediation, a subject I will return to in later chapters.

Differentiation: Basic and Functional

The third central Bowen theory concept, and perhaps Bowen's most important theoretical notion, is that of differentiation. Differentiation is a complex theoretical concept. It is the interplay and expression between the individuality and togetherness life forces in action. It is the capacity for self-definition and self-regulation. It is being one's own person, while remaining authentically and intimately connected to others. It is the ability to self-reflect; thoughtfully self-manage one's thinking, feelings, and behavior; clearly define a self; and effectively connect with others. Differentiation is not static interpersonally or intrapersonally; rather, it is individualistic (one person is more differentiated than some and less differentiated than others) and dynamic within individuals (depending on the level of stress within a person's current life circumstances). While one's *basic differentiation* is an outcome of many factors, including that which is emotionally "inherited" from one's family, it tends to remain fairly static throughout life unless one actively works to increase it, life circumstance offers ample opportunities to enhance one's capacity for adaptation, or challenges are so overwhelming as to create permanent regression.

In contrast, a person's *functional differentiation* changes as a result of the stresses and strains she is experiencing. For example, Claire has lived a fortunate life in that she is in a relatively calm and stable environment. As a result, Claire appears very emotionally healthy and differentiated. Recently, however, Claire lost her job and her mother has taken critically ill. As these pressures increase, Claire becomes more reactive and emotional. She looks less capable of adapting to her life circumstances and begins drinking more to relieve the pressures in her life. Her functional differentiation decreases in reaction to these external pressures and crises. The higher a person's basic differentiation, the less change in functional differentiation over time and across situations. A person's "core" level of emotional maturity inoculates her from some of the negative effects of stress. The lower a person's basic differentiation, the more change in functional differentiation over time and across situations. Claire, as an example of a person with a lower level of basic differentiation, struggles to manage her life circumstances in the face of increasing stress and uncertainty.

Differentiation can be conceptualized on a theoretical scale from 0 to 100 (Kerr and Bowen, 1988). On this scale, 0 represent a person without any sense of self, capacity to self-regulate, or ability to relate to others. It is a theoretical position, as most people have some capacity in these categories. A 100 on the scale represents a person who can fully self-regulate, has a completely developed sense of self, and can relate to all people in all circumstances. Again, this is a theoretical position, since even the most emotionally mature person is not perfect. In fact, even the most self-differentiated humans are likely to only approach 65-75 on this scale. The scale's usefulness is as a theoretical tool, one that conceptualizes human functioning as being on a continuum, with different people falling at different points on the scale. Bowen's scale of differentiation helps us appreciate the diversity of human functioning and the complexity of factors that influence the expression of human behavior. Synonyms for differentiation include emotional maturity, personal integrity, ability to adapt to life's various situations and challenges, and willingness to accept personal responsibility for one's being and destiny (Friedman, 1991, 1996; Kerr and Bowen, 1988).

Other researchers and theoreticians have hypothesized notions similar to Bowen's concept of differentiation. Howard Gardner's (1983, 1993) theory of multiple intelligences examines the importance of the personal intelligences—the interpersonal intelligence and the intrapersonal intelligence—in successful life development. Gardner and others have proposed, through theory and research, that developing the personal intelligences can create favorable climates for learning and development. Martin Buber (2000), a German-Jewish religious scholar and philosopher, spoke about the "I-Thou" relationship, emphasizing the importance of the response between the "you" in relationship to the "me." Daniel Goleman (1994, 2006) and his associates have written extensively about and conducted research on emotional intelligence, an intelligence that sounds remarkably like Bowen's differentiation and Gardner's personal intelligences. Emotional intelligence is the capacity to self-regulate and know oneself as well as the capacity to understand and manage others.

For these theoreticians, effective functioning in life is largely dependent on the expression of these twin variables: developing the self (defining an "I" that is different from the "we"), taking personal responsibility for one's behaviors and actions, committing to greater self-regulation or self-management, and developing important relationships with others. Connecting with others has a great deal to do with empathy and compassion, behaving altruistically, knowing how to get along with others individually and in groups without compromising self, and nurturing deep, intimate relationships with significant others.

A more highly differentiated person is more adaptive. She is less reactive; her responses are more consistent, autonomous, and thoughtful in a variety of stressful situations; and she is more emotionally free, thus more capable of responding to different situations with diverse responses. She is spontaneous, has more resources, and can express her feelings and thoughts more articulately. In essence, the more highly differentiated person is a more emotionally mature person, an individual willing, as Friedman (1996) suggests, "to take responsibility for (her) emotional being and destiny" (p. 16).

In contrast, a less differentiated person has fewer resources and is less adaptive. Like a rubber band stretched too often, he reacts more automatically and lacks resiliency to bounce back from stressful encounters. He is less emotionally free, and his reactivity can take many forms, including reactive thinking, reactive feeling, and reactive behavior. He is less focused on his own internal compass and thus less capable of taking personal responsibility. His impulse is to criticize others and get them to change. He is also more influenced by those in his present and past. He uses relationship *cutoff, emotional distance,* and *triangulation* (key Bowen theory concepts) to manage conflict, and he tends to fault others for his life circumstances.

The differentiation levels of both the mediators and the disputants are central to mediation success. Principally, the level of emotional maturity of the mediators, in particular, may be the single most significant variable in determining success or failure in mediation. Because the role of differentiation in the mediation process is the most important concept in Bowen theory, I will examine it more extensively in Chapter 5: "Emotional Maturity and the Mediator."

Chronic Anxiety

A fourth central concept in Bowen theory is *chronic anxiety*. Chronic anxiety can be thought of as the flip side of differentiation. Chronic anxiety is the degree to which a person reacts to a *perceived* threat (Kerr and Bowen, 1988). Chronic anxiety is different than acute anxiety, a more surface anxiety akin to reactions to *actual* threat. Like differentiation, chronic anxiety is something humans share with all living creatures since all organisms constantly react to changes in their environments and threats to their existence. As such, chronic anxiety is more commensurate with the evolutionarily older emotional system, and it is inversely related to a person's degree of differentiation. That is, the greater a person's capacity for self-definition and self-regulation, the lower his level of chronic anxiety. As chronic anxiety increases, an individual's capacity for self-definition and self-management decreases. Chronic anxiety is also a multifactor concept. A person's level of chronic anxiety is related to the degree of chronic anxiety in her parents, which is related to the amount of chronic anxiety in the multigenerational system. These levels predispose each person to transmit chronic anxiety through physical, emotional, and/or social symptoms; again, these expressions are also related to the manifestation of chronic anxiety in the nuclear and extended family. In other words, certain patterns from current and previous generations, which are a function of biological factors such as gene expression and environmental influences such as current and historical stressors, will affect how each person absorbs, manages, and expresses chronic anxiety. The manifestation of chronic anxiety through emotional reactivity is of critical importance in all interactions with the human and non-human world. The lower an individual's tolerance for ambiguity, emotional intensity, and perceived threats, the lower his level of differentiation and the higher his level of chronic anxiety.

In mediation, disputants arrive in a heightened state of emotional intensity, so they attend mediation with their anxiety aroused and their predisposed ways of managing acute and chronic anxiety exposed. In addition to the differentiation levels of the participants, the levels of chronic anxiety become crucial variables in mediation success and failure. In future chapters, I will discuss how to manage chronic anxiety in mediation, focusing particularly on the way in which disputants become anxiously attached to not only their positions but to the conflict itself.

Emotional Triangles

The fifth and final central concept of Bowen theory that is relevant to mediators and mediation is that of the *emotional triangle*. Bowen said that for humans the basic emotional building block is the triangle. In essence, he observed that a two-person relationship is inherently unstable and will, under stress, automatically seek to re-stabilize itself by bringing in a third. This re-stabilization attempt is called *triangulation* or *triangling*. This third point on the emotional triangle can be another person, such as a child or an affair within a marriage. A twosome may, however, triangulate a physical object (money, house, pet, or other possession). Triangulation can also occur through a variety of other forms such as substances (alcohol, food, or drugs), belief system (religion, political conviction, or "cause"), and other attachments. Recognizing the universality of the triangle, of course, is not new. Many cultures believe in archetypal symbols, which, in addition to the triangle, have included the cross, circle, square, and other two-dimensional motifs as well as three-dimensional objects and symbols, such as the sphere, cube, and pyramid. For Bowen, though, the triangle was the most important symbol of human functioning (Kerr and Bowen, 1988).

In Bowen family systems theory, the sides of the triangle are conduits through which emotional energy or anxiety flows. The distance or closeness between any two people in an emotional triangle designates which two are on the inside position of the triangle and which one is on the outside position of the triangle. Those on the inside position keep their closeness by keeping the third out. For example, Lee and Jayla work together in a small business. Lee's annual evaluation is conducted by his supervisor, Alicia. Alicia's review finds performance problems with Lee, especially his chronic tardiness. Lee's level of differentiation is moderately low. As a result, instead of taking personal responsibility for this identified performance deficit, or addressing his concerns about the evaluation directly to Alicia, Lee complains about being unfairly treated to Jayla. Jayla expresses sympathy and outrage to Lee; Lee, in turn, feels validated by Jayla. Lee and Jayla are on the inside position of the emotional triangle, while Alicia is on the outside position. Lee feels better, Jayla feels worse, and Alicia is oblivious about Lee's concerns and thus cannot assist him in resolving his issues. The matter is not resolved. In fact, Lee feels better at the expense of his relationship with Alicia and his ability to correct an identified work performance concern.

If conflict or tension increases between two individuals on the inside position of an emotional triangle, one person may move closer to the person on the outside position of the triangle in order to reduce conflict. This creates a new inside position with the third person, originally on the inside, now on the outside (Kerr and Bowen, 1988). For example, Jayla begins to realize that

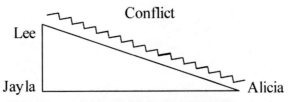

Figure 2.1.   Lee, Jayla, & Alicia Central Triangle.

Lee's chronic tardiness affects her ability to get her work completed. When Jayla tries to speak with Lee about this, Lee expresses outrage at Jayla. Jayla, instead of holding her ground in an attempt to resolve the conflict, complains to Alicia, who expresses her own frustration about Lee to Jayla. Now, Jayla and Alicia occupy the inside positions of the emotional triangle and Lee inhabits the outside position. As none of the parties are taking responsibility for managing the conflict, their triangling creates temporary stability through shifting alliances but does nothing to improve the relationship between the parties. In fact, the relationships deteriorate through the shifting inside and outside positions.

Emotional triangles and triangulation are dynamic and complicated processes. A central emotional triangle, one within which the "core" conflict is locked, will form *interlocking triangles* when stressed further and when anxiety needs additional places to flow. That is, if a particular emotional triangle "overheats" with conflict such that the anxiety in the three-person system can no longer be contained, someone else may be brought in to help temporarily stabilize the system. These triangulation processes are automatic and so not usually under conscious control. To continue with the above example, Alicia, having been riled up by Jayla, loudly complains to her supervisor, Byron. Byron, having experienced problems with Lee before, and having never addressed those concerns directly to Lee through an improvement plan when he directly supervised Lee, bonds with Alicia over Lee's ineptitude. An interlocking emotional triangle catches the anxiety that "spills" out of the central triangle of Lee-Jayla-Alicia. Again, the relationship conflicts shift between the parties without adequate resolution.

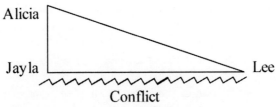

Figure 2.2.   Alicia, Jayla, & Lee Triangle.

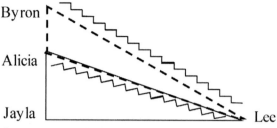

Figure 2.3.   Interlocking Triangle.

The emotional energy flowing through emotional triangles is chronic anxiety. When chronic anxiety attaches itself to a person, object, substance, symptom, or idea, it is called *anxiety binding*. Anxiety binders are ways in which people who get reactive with one another stay connected through their attachment to the conflict. This triangulation process, since it does not resolve the conflict but only binds it in temporary relief, decreases the participants' capacity for independent and thoughtful functioning, as is the case with all of the participants: Lee, Jayla, Alicia, and Byron.

Triangulation occurs when a conflict or disagreement between two people is not contained and resolved between the two through calm, focused dialogue that results in solutions that lessen the conflict and thus the stress. Rather, as the stress between the two grows and the disagreement is not adequately managed, someone or something else is brought in to temporarily stabilize the situation. For example, two business partners seek to expand their business and want to hire a new employee. Partner Juanita wants to hire Sierra, and Partner Salvador does not. Long-standing disagreements, unaired and unresolved, become coagulated around the hire, and the partners solidify their positions around this issue, so that the conflict is now more about the hire than the differences between their business practices. Sierra becomes triangled into their relationship, and the anxiety between Juanita and Salvador gets detoured through and "bound" to Sierra. Sierra becomes the anxiety binder for the business partners' conflict.

Another example of triangulation is illustrated in a case I mediated. The conflict was between a homebuilder, Ansell, and a homeowner, Jim. The case came to mediation because of several disputes around the quality of the construction, specifically cracks in the concrete driveway and a leak in the bathroom that was dripping through the basement. These relatively minor concerns had escalated into a major lawsuit. In mediation, it was clear that there had been a number of vicious verbal altercations between Ansell and Jim during the construction of the home, with allegations of incompetence, contract violations over materials used in the project, and intentional delays in completing the project. As the two men were unable to civilly and calmly discuss, negotiate, and resolve these concerns as they developed, a reservoir of bad feelings had built up. When these relatively minor problems surfaced, the anxiety between the two became crystallized or "bound" in the concrete flaws and the leak. Each party became reactive to the other, attached to being wronged by the other, and rigidly locked into his position. The dispute itself became the anxiety binder for Ansell and Jim, and neither was initially capable of moving from his anxiety-bound position to common interests.

In fact, this is a common thread in most disputes that reach the courts and mediation: disputants become attached to their positions and the issues comprising the dispute, and the dispute itself becomes the anxiety binder that "locks" the parties into the rightness of their actions and beliefs, thus perpetuating and aggravating the conflict. By definition, then, the parties in mediation are triangulated by the conflict and their positions. The emotional flow of anxiety is bound up in the issue, person, or thing being mediated. The issue, person, or thing, then, becomes the anxiety binder for the parties.

In mediation, each party is usually vying for the inside position of the triangle with the third point of the triangle, the issue or dispute itself, as the anxiety binder. In a second mediation example, two business partners, Rafael and Donna wanted to dissolve their corporation. They got stuck over distribution of resources, current employees for the new company they each wanted to form, and the company name. All became anxiety binders whereby emotional attachments created positional stances, distracting them from interest-based negotiations.

The stronger the degree of attachment or *fusion* with the anxiety binder, the more the person's self is wrapped up in and invested with the anxiety binder, which, in turn, makes it more difficult to reach a mediated solution. Positions become hardened and impasses more likely.

Triangulation, then, is a self-propelling process by which anxiety moves through a system. It is an automatic way in which two people in conflict bring in a third "other" to help lower the anxiety of the system, attain temporary relief from the suffering that conflict brings, and attempt to achieve greater temporary balance and re-stabilization. Unfortunately, any initial benefits brought about by triangulation are usually short lived. Automatic reactivity tends to escalate, and these temporary attempts to decrease short-term anxiety usually lead to increases in long-term emotional reactivity and de-stabilization of the two-person relationship system.

Related to the theoretical concepts of emotional triangles, triangulation, and anxiety binders is the concept of de-triangulation. De-triangulation occurs when a person rejects the negative option to perpetuate a conflict through triangling and anxiety binding. Instead, de-triangulation is a method by which one can reduce conflict through clearheaded thinking and acting. In de-triangulation, the person strives toward a more differentiated response, rather than perpetuating emotional reactivity. Attempts at de-triangulation are efforts at increasing one's level of differentiation. In de-triangling from an emotionally intense situation, the person must reflect on the current situation, manage her reactivity to the situation, take personal responsibility for her part in the problem, and interact respectfully with the other party in an effort to find common ground through their common interests. De-triangulation, therefore, is a critical concept in mediation. For a mediator, de-triangulating the disputants from their attachment to the conflict means approaching the parties with respect, making a concerted effort to connect equally with each party, keeping good humor to avoid a "reptilian regression" into rigid, un-yielding seriousness and attachment to positions, and fostering a non-anxious mediation triangle. These mediation applications are discussed more fully in subsequent chapters.

In all human interactions, the key to managing emotional triangles and anxiety is to tolerate short-term anxiety increases for the sake of long-term anxiety reduction and relief (Kerr and Bowen, 1988; Lerner, 1989). Address-ing conflict directly often generates more initial anxiety than ignoring, dis-placing, or detouring the conflict and complaining to another. In mediation, this means keeping the parties in contact with a mediator who is minimally reactive to the reactivity of the disputants, moderately to highly differenti-ated, and calm. If this occurs, the disputants can seek interest-based alterna-tives to the current conflict without resorting to habitual, positional patterns of reacting and blaming.

While Bowen family system theory has additional central and secondary concepts, including nuclear family emotional process, multigenerational emotional process, and societal emotional process, the essential concepts relevant to mediation include the emotional system, individuality and togeth-erness, differentiation, chronic anxiety, and the emotional triangle.

In summary, the concept of the emotional system connects humans with all biotic life. It suggests that most human behavior is rooted in evolutionary older structures and functions that predate the development of thinking or feeling. The emotional system, in effect, represents our instinctual, automatic reactions, especially in stressful situations. Individuality and togetherness are complementary life forces that are expressions of the emotional system, and they determine the degree to which we can live as separate individuals, while remaining genuinely bonded to others. Differentiation or emotional maturity is our capacity to regulate our thinking, feelings, and actions, as well as our ability to clearly define who we are and what we want in the world. Differentiation also includes our capacity to cultivate relationships that strengthen each member in that relationship. Chronic anxiety is our reaction to perceived threats. It is inversely related to differentiation, such that as emotional maturity increases, chronic anxiety decreases, and as differentiation decreases, chronic anxiety increases. The more chronic anxiety a person carries, the higher the degree of emotional reactivity, especially under stressful encounters. Emotional triangles are natural ways that chronic anxiety is managed through detouring attention from the source of the threat to another person, object, belief, or thing. Emotional triangles temporarily relieve the anxiety of the moment by binding that anxiety in someone or something else. The greater the triangulation, the more differentiation is compromised. De-triangulation manages the anxiety of the moment by addressing it directly. While this is initially less comfortable, de-triangulation provides people with the opportunity to find long-term solutions to chronic and acute problems by promoting personal responsibility, compassion, and genuine dialogue regarding conflict and its resolution. De-triangling *is* differentiating.

All of these Bowen theory concepts are interrelated and all are pertinent to mediation. In subsequent chapters, I will expand on these crucial variables. Then, I will apply Bowen theory to mediation and demonstrate its effectiveness as a theoretical system in understanding and influencing personal behavior and the behavior of others.

The next chapter applies Bowen theory through the six-stage North American model of mediation.

Part II

MEDIATION PROCESS AND TECHNIQUE USING BOWEN THEORY

Chapter Three

Applying Bowen Theory to the Six-Stage Model of Mediation

This chapter addresses the six stages of mediation specific to the North American model, how Bowen theory re-conceptualizes the stages, and how the practitioner can use theory as a way to effectively manage the emotional climate in mediation.

UNDERLYING ASSUMPTIONS AND UNDERSTANDINGS

Mediation usually occurs within a highly anxious environment as disputants enter the mediation already in conflict. That conflict ranges on a continuum from mild to severe. Generally, mediations are fraught with anxiety as the parties come to mediation with their emotions running high. Parties either reluctantly attend mediation voluntarily, often without much hope of a positive outcome, or they are ordered by the courts to attempt mediation before they can present their cases before a judge. In either scenario, disputants are often unenthusiastic and suspicious attendees. In this intense emotional field, functional differentiation is usually diminished as the parties' ability to self-focus, accept personal responsibility for their role in the conflict, and self-manage their reactions are compromised. More often, the disputants each build up their own positions at the expense of each other, rather than objectively looking for a reasonable solution that meets the interests of both parties.

The biology of high arousal from the limbic system makes matters worse (Atkinson, 1999; Goleman, 2006). The limbic system is a remarkable structure that has protected the human species for countless millennia. In highly anxious environments, the limbic system is usually activated such that the brain's fight-flight center, the amygdala (or what I referred to as the "reptilian" brain), is in a state of heightened arousal. Once triggered, a person's innate reactions are to flee, fight, or freeze. Unfortunately, limbic activation can also be auto-matic or "mindless"; that is, amygdala engagement can undercut thoughtful-ness, calmness, and the capacity to engage higher-order thinking. Clearheaded thinking is often compromised in such a highly-aroused condition. In this primitive, emotional state, parties are prepared to defend themselves or fight it out in mediation, thus replicating the very problematic processes that likely led to the disintegration of the working or marital relationship and the disagree-ments related to the dispute itself.

With the executive functions of the brain highjacked, critical operations for developing agreements—such as foresight, planning, judgment, and other fu-ture-oriented thinking—suffer. It is in this highly reactive, emotional environ-ment that mediation is typically convened. Knowing the neurology of arousal, however, can assist mediators in promoting a calm emotional environment that provides safety, develops trust, and encourages disputants to think more clearly using the higher functioning, pre-frontal, cortical components of their brains. In sum, calming the brain's fight-flight center improves the parties' capacity to think and act more rationally, thus minimizing emotional fighting and fleeing reactions.

Understanding of the biology of arousal is helpful for the mediator, as she can better enter mediation in a more objective capacity, as an emotional bal-ancer. The skill of the mediator as unbiased facilitator is paramount to an ef-fective mediation process. Often, disputants enter mediation leveling charges of incompetence and mistreatment at one another. Hyper-arousal is common, and the parties begin verbally accosting each other in mediation, or else one party attempts to flee by rejecting mediation or refusing to participate in the same room with the other party. Also, a mediator can become affected by the disputants' anxieties, as emotionality is infectious (Goleman, 2006). This may, in turn, decrease the mediator's capacity to remain more neutral and balanced (Regina, 2000).

In an emotionally-charged environment such as this, the mediator's clarity and calmness are the best safeguards for helping the participants discover and unlock the best interests of both parties. The mediator is most effective if *he* maintains calm, stays deeply committed to the process and stages of mediation, and remains non-attached to the form of the outcome. Understand-ing Bowen theory helps tremendously with this process. Conceptualizing conflict management in terms of decreasing emotional arousal, promoting clearheaded thinking in oneself and others, as well as comprehending and managing the dynamics of brain physiology, allows the mediator to proceed with greater clarity, confidence, and core sense of self. In effect, the mediator can influence the disputants and thus the mediation itself through his more differentiated presence. As the leader in the mediation system, the mediator's ability to "see systems" helps him understand what is happening, connect with each participant in an effort to shift the reactivity away from the escalation of conflict, and remain more objective about the importance of personal self-regulation. Goleman, Boyatzis, and McKee (2002) and Friedman (2007) note that the leader in any system has a heightened ability to influence the emotional tone of any interaction. Working on one's own differentiation as a mediator has profound implications for the entire mediation process. I will discuss this more extensively in Chapter 5.

THE SIX STAGES OF MEDIATION AND BOWEN THEORY

Stage I: Introductions

Convening the mediation sets the stage for the entire process. Even before beginning the mediation, however, there are important decisions to address. For example, what happens if one party, or both, brings an attorney? How might Bowen theory guide the mediator in this circumstance even before the disputants sit down together? Attorneys can be helpful in mediation, acting as a disputant's "rational mind" during the mediation. This is especially true with high-conflict disputants and when attorneys are trained in mediation or familiar with the benefits of mediation. Attorneys can assist their clients in examining their Best Alternative to a Negotiated Agreement (BATNA) and their Worst Alternative to a Negotiated Agreement (WATNA). In domestic mediations, attorneys can also be allies for children, helping clients stay focused on their children's best interests. Attorneys can also undercut the mediation process, especially if they are not trained in mediation, not familiar with the benefits of mediation, or pre-disposed to wanting to fight it out in court.

Jeff Kichaven (2005), a mediator from Los Angeles, asserts that it is best to meet separately with each disputant and her attorney *before* convening the formal mediation. I find that meeting with each attorney and client prior to bringing the disputants together has several advantages. From a Bowen theory perspective, this initial meeting allows me to define the mediation process and the roles and functions of the mediator, disputants, and attorneys to all parties. Completing this procedure separately with each subgroup assists me in establishing a relational connection with the disputants and the attorneys, while effectively managing the beginning stage of the mediation process. If I have worked with an attorney previously and the experience has been positive, this relationship building and role clarification process is not as crucial. Even if I am familiar with the attorney, though, this initial meeting helps the disputant understand the expectations for herself and her attorney.

I have successfully experimented with an effective alternative, which is meeting with the attorneys together before convening the mediation. This strategy reinforces the professional roles of mediators and attorneys. It also educates attorneys about the mediation process, their roles in the mediation, my responsibility, and the importance of the disputants' self-determination in resolving their own conflict. With both strategies, I make clear that the attorneys' job is to observe and speak when I ask them to speak, consult with their clients should they or their clients feel the need to talk, and allow the disputants to develop a working agreement consistent with their best interests.

An initial meeting is even more important if I have worked with an attorney previously and the attorney's presence has not been productive. If an attorney tends to dominate, is contentious, or in other ways has undercut the mediation process, this separate meeting to clarify goals, roles, expectations, and procedures allows me to firmly establish control of the mediation process. In fact, I mention to the attorneys that there may come a time in mediation, after all of the legal issues have been addressed, when the attorneys are dismissed in order to give the parties an opportunity to complete the mediation on their own. I use this as a "fail-safe" mechanism whereby I position myself as having the authority to dismiss disruptive attorneys without having to engage in a power struggle with them. This face-saving statement is reinforced in the *Agreement to Participate in Mediation* form that our court system uses, which is signed by the disputants and the attorneys. The document states: "During the mediation process, if we choose to have our lawyers present, they will be expected to follow the rules established for this mediation by the mediators." Fortunately, our local rule gives mediators this authority.

If I have not worked with an attorney previously, I can clarify the roles and responsibilities of each party and answer any questions the attorney or client may have about the expectations and procedures in the mediation process. From a Bowen theory perspective, it is easier to manage disagreements and conflicts within these subgroups before assembling everyone together. The likelihood of attorneys and clients reacting to boundaries that define and guide the mediation process decreases if the other disputant is not present. In other words, it is easier to establish a working relationship with all parties if I can focus one-on-one with the disputant and attorney team, or alternatively the two attorneys together without their clients, rather than having to manage these issues in a larger setting with more people and thus more opportunity for limbic activation, attorney and client posturing, and emotional triangulation. Ultimately, escalating conflict and triangulation are less likely when I establish a strong, clear relationship with all of the parties from the beginning.

Also, if one party brings an attorney and the other party does not, there is a natural power imbalance. I meet with the participant and attorney first and then with the unrepresented party. I can often assuage the second party's anxiety by assuring her that the attorney will not be allowed to dominate and control the process. I clarify for the unrepresented party the limited role of the attorney, thus attempting to re-balance the mediation. Sometimes the unrepresented party is adamant that the attorney not attend the mediation. If I am unsuccessful in assuring the unrepresented participant that the attorney's role is secondary, and that the parties are responsible for the mediation and crafting an agreement, I dismiss the attorney. This helps ensure that emotional safety, balance, and fairness are maintained. Again, from a Bowen theory perspective, these decisions are best discussed and managed in smaller subgroups to minimize feelings of anger, disappointment, fear, and embarrassment, therefore minimizing the possibility of hyper-arousal, chronic anxiety flooding, and thus emotional triangulation.

Bowen theory frames this strategy from the perspective of differentiation. That is, I am in charge of the mediation. I am the leader of the process and, as such, I am charged with establishing an effective emotional atmosphere to maximize success. This is best accomplished through a more differentiated response: the twin capacities of self-definition/self-regulation and connecting with others. By clearly defining the expectations of the parties in mediation, the roles and responsibilities of disputants, attorneys, and mediators, managing my own reactivity to the emotional reactivity of the disputants and attorneys, and being able to effectively build a working relationship with all involved in the mediation, I have effectively negotiated the first barrier to reaching a working agreement with the parties. I can maximize the chances of reaching this and future agreements if I have been clear, direct, personable, and strong regarding who is in charge of the mediation and what the expectations and procedures are in mediation.

If I conduct pre-mediation meetings with attorney and client subgroups, I present the entire introduction to each subgroup. Discussing the stages of mediation, the guidelines/ground rules, answering questions, reading the consent agreement, and having each disputant and attorney sign the agreement to participate help establish the framework for an effective mediation.

If attorneys are not present, I implement the introduction stage more traditionally, with both disputants in the same room. During the introduction, I seek to define the mediation process, clarify the roles and responsibilities of each party, answer questions, read and sign the consent agreement, and establish guidelines/ground rules. While these are the same steps for most mediators in the introduction stage, Bowen theory helps the mediator understand the meta-process in this stage.

A clear and concise introduction helps calm the participants. For many disputants, mediation is an unknown arena. They come to mediation suspicious, anxious, and unsure about what to expect. Delineating the process of mediation, articulating the stages of mediation, reviewing the expectations and procedures, and clarifying guidelines/ground rules help remove the uncertainty about mediation, allowing the parties to begin minimizing defenses and relaxing into the process. Also, effective introductions help create rapport, establish me as expert guide in the process, promote safety, and develop trust. The formal introduction is the first opportunity I have for developing a more differentiated connection with the disputants and assessing their capacity to effectively work together.

When disputants enter mediation in a heightened state of arousal, their anxiety levels are elevated and can manifest through reactive thinking (self-justifications, blaming, and rationalizing behavior or goals), reactive feelings (distrust, suspicion, fear, anger, and even hatred), and emotionally activated fight-flight reactions. If I emanate a calm demeanor, exhibit clarity of thinking and expectations, demonstrate the capacity to remain non-judgmental, and show compassion for and commitment to both parties, I begin the process of building a mediation triangle with the parties. As the leader in the mediation process, I help quiet the emotional system so that the parties have a chance to more thoughtfully discuss the matters before them.

Proponents of Bowen theory understand how the brain works. In particular, we know that appropriate humor is one of the most effective tools to calm the highly aroused limbic brain. As such, mediators are well advised to use appropriate humor as both a diagnostic tool and as a mechanism to relieve and dispel anxiety. When people laugh, they tend to calm down the more emotionally charged parts of their brains. Using appropriate humor with disputants helps them relax, re-focuses their energies in more appropriate ways, and promotes clearer thinking. Conversely, if disputants cannot laugh at appropriate humor, it informs me that the participants are probably in a highly aroused state and are less likely to be able to manage their overwhelming reactivity.

Stage II: Uninterrupted Time

From a Bowen theory perspective, Stage II, or "uninterrupted time," is perhaps the most important stage in the mediation process. Uninterrupted time allows each disputant to tell his or her story to me without disruption from the other participant. Traditionally, uninterrupted time is conceptualized as a way for each disputant to explain the situation, to express her/his feelings about what has occurred, and to present what she/he hopes to accomplish in the mediation.

Bowen theory mediators conceptualize this stage in a similar manner. The crucial distinction between more traditionally trained mediators and those trained in Bowen theory is that, from the onset, Bowen theory mediators frame this stage as important for the *mediator*. That is, during the introduction and again at the beginning of Stage II, I emphasize that uninterrupted time allows me to understand the participants' unique situations and stories. The emphasis is based on the assumption that I can best help the parties if I understand the participants and the situation, as each person perceives it. This is a *definitional reframe* highlighting the importance of the *relationship* between the mediator and the disputants, rather than the mediator simply listening to their stories as a fact-finding mission. Uninterrupted time deepens the important processes of building trust, promoting safety, and developing rapport. In essence, the good will and empathic connections established during uninterrupted time foster the development of the mediation triangle.

The concept of the mediation triangle highlights several aspects of Bowen theory important in mediation. First, most participants come to mediation highly attached to specific positions. These positions have to do with the status of being wronged by the other and wanting to right that wrong through a specific course of remedial action. A central goal in mediation is to help disputants shift from positions, which are fixed expectations that are largely a function of anxiety binding, to more flexible interests, which highlight the underlying needs of the parties. By definition, the issues in dispute (contract violations, custody disputes, offender crimes, etc.) are anxiety binders and, as such, the parties are initially not able to uncover their interests because of their positional attachments. Each participant and the issue form the central triangle, and the parties will automatically seek to triangulate the mediator into the conflict. While this, of course, is not in their best interest in promoting a clearheaded solution and finding common and non-overlapping interests, triangling is a reflexive process. In fact, Bowen theory presupposes that triangulation is automatic in all relationships, that is, everyone triangulates to greater and lesser degrees, and that the more intensity around the conflict the higher the anxiety and the more rigid the triangulation process. How then does one de-triangulate the disagreements and issues from this intense emotional field? I have conceptualized the concept of a *mediation triangle* to assist with this important process. In a mediation triangle, I form the third point on the triangle with the two parties. Without absorbing the anxiety of the conflict, a mediation triangle shifts the emotional intensity away from the issues and onto the relationship with me. This promotes less reactive and more thoughtful responding by the parties.

During uninterrupted time, I am restating, empathically responding and summarizing, detoxifying language, reframing positions to interests, asking clarification questions, and, most importantly, establishing rapport with each party. To effectively create a mediation triangle, I must relate *equally* to both participants or else I risk getting triangled into the conflict on one side or the other. During Stage II, I re-direct anxiety from the issues and the other party to me. It is essential that I not "absorb" the anxiety of the parties, but rather provide a forum for the disputants to be recognized and heard. For the mediation triangle to succeed, both parties must feel heard, understood, and connected to the mediator by the end of Stage II. Like an equilateral triangle (a triangle with equal sides), the mediator must strive to develop and strengthen each side of the mediation triangle uniformly with both parties. This process is the same whether the mediator is working solo or with a co-mediator.

It should be noted that working with a co-mediator presents additional challenges, and I will discuss these challenges in Chapter 5, *Emotional Maturity and the Mediator*. In general, though, it is crucial that the co-mediators understand the importance of establishing the mediation triangle by not becoming a part of the disputants' conflict through side-taking or other behaviors that undercut the objectivity and balance of the team. In fact, if the co-mediators are not equally aware of and committed to the task of forming a mediation triangle, the mediation process is undercut with the likelihood of developing an effective agreement diminished.

For example, Scarlett, age 15, was arrested for assaulting Tamara, age 16, at the county fair. This dispute was simmering at the high school for months. Each girl believed that the other had it in for her. Their peer group had also split up and the girls were leaders of the two factions. As a result, the other girls pushed and escalated the conflict between Scarlett and Tamara. Name calling, obscene phone calls to each other's homes, escalating threats of violence, and shoving matches accelerated into a full-blown physical fight at the fairground, with Scarlett pulling a knife on Tamara. The police were called and Scarlett was arrested, since she had brandished the weapon. Fortunately, neither girl was hurt badly, so the juvenile court judge referred the case to victim-offender mediation. When the girls arrived with their mothers, all parties were in a state of heightened arousal. None of the participants wanted to attend mediation, each side blamed the other side for the escalation and the violence, and neither side was receptive to accepting any responsibility for the rising conflict.

My co-mediator, Heather, had pre-screened the disputants, informing them about the mediation process and our expectations for their participation. Despite pre-mediation case development that included Scarlett admitting wrongdoing for brandishing the knife at Tamara, when the parties arrived at the mediation, they were hostile and guarded. After securing their agreements to participate and completing the other important components in Stage I, we allowed each party, mothers and daughters alike, to tell their stories. When one of the participants would stray from the tight parameters of telling us her story by turning to the other side and raising her voice or blaming the others, we calmly re-directed her back to telling us her story. When the other side attempted to interrupt the storyteller by disagreeing with her or accusing her of distorting the facts, we blocked the intruder, assuring her that she would have ample time to fully tell us her side of the tale. At every turn, we assured the parties that we knew little about the conflict and the only way that we could help them was if we were able to listen to and understand their stories directly.

This focus on *our* need to listen to their tales uninterrupted allowed us, as co-mediators, to not only contain the conflict within acceptable boundaries but also to develop rapport with all four participants so that they knew that we cared about helping them find an acceptable resolution to their conflict. Closely collaborating with each other as co-mediators, Heather and I were able to calm the disputants, demonstrate our competence in managing their emotional intensity, deal with their concerns, establish working relationships with each party based on empathy and content reflection, detoxify their language, and begin the crucial movement from positions to interests.

Stage III: The Exchange

Having successfully encouraged the parties to tell their stories, express their feelings, and describe what it is they wish to accomplish through mediation, the participants are better situated to begin working together to discuss their concerns more rationally and to explore common interests.

Traditionally in Stage III, "the exchange," the mediator shifts the focus to the disputants and has them begin conversing directly with each other. During the exchange, the disputants enter into a discussion focused on their feelings about the issues and explore what they want from the mediation. The mediator facilitates dialogue, continually reframes through detoxifying harsh language, promotes flexible interests rather than rigid positions, and acknowledges success at communication. A key goal of the exchange is to respectfully air differences, vent feelings, and begin the process of developing a mutual understanding of each other.

I find that occasionally, low-conflict parties or a more differentiated participant will bring outlines of an interest-based resolution to mediation. These outlines can serve as a beginning point for crafting an agreement. Understanding the importance of working together for their common interests, low-conflict participants and more differentiated parties are ready and willing to cooperate. They are less attached to the dispute, can place their differences in perspective, and are ready to move on. Sometimes, one participant is more willing and able than the other. When in this situation, I find that it is important to continue to engage each party and avoid taking sides with the more emotionally mature participant. The effectiveness of the exchange is predicated on my continuing to develop and strengthen the mediation triangle, which, by definition, necessitates that I connect equally with both participants. If both parties are so inclined to work cooperatively, this indicates a level of differentiation that is higher than disputants with elevated chronic anxiety and thus higher conflict. While the importance of rapport building and developing a mediation triangle is important with low-conflict disputants as well, these people are best served by me staying out of their way and not impeding their developing capacity to work together.

When working with medium-conflict and high-conflict disputants, including those parties where one person is more highly capable and one person is less capable and adaptable, I must remain more actively involved. The groundwork of building rapport through the mediation triangle, successfully established in Stage II, allows each party in this stage to feel understood, valued, and not judged. I am thus freer to probe, challenge, reframe, support, acknowledge, and confront participants as they temporarily accept me into their conflict. Throughout the process, I use appropriate humor to enter the participants' worlds, loosen the stranglehold of rigid attachments to positions, and aid the parties to find and develop their common interests.

In my experience, the most crucial function of the mediator is to help calm the system by remaining calm. In essence, soothing the parties promotes clear thinking, creative problem solving, and the capacity to work cooperatively. Stage II success helps lower anxiety and encourages dialogue in Stage III that allows for more responsible sharing of feelings and perspectives, as well as exploring interests over positions. As the parties experience connection and success, they begin to relax. This positive feedback loop reinforces constructive change.

In Stage III, I request that each disputant use "I language," that is, each participant is asked to speak for herself and himself. Each person is encouraged to clarify important issues rather than to blame or interpret the actions of the other party. Bowen theorist, practitioner, and feminist Harriet Lerner (1989) says that "I language" is the language of personal responsibility. It fosters self-differentiation, as the emphasis shifts from other-focused reactivity and blaming to self-focused thoughtfulness and accountability. In addition, I challenge each party to concentrate on what he/she is willing to do to promote personal responsibility. I emphasize that the only person one can control is oneself. That is, I highlight that "other-focused" thinking, feeling, and reacting, such as blaming and accusing, are ultimately self-defeating as it shifts personal empowerment to the other party. I offer self-focus, self-definition, and self-management as an alternative means to developing and promoting personal power.

Successfully negotiating this stage is important for creating the context for developing a successful mediation agreement. To the degree that I have been effective in joining with the participants in an equal and balanced manner, I can actively enter the discussions or leave the parties to their own exchanges, depending on the disputants, the topics, and the situations. Having developed a repository of good will, I can "cash in" my relationship capital with the parties. While I do not decide on the specifics of an agreement, a solid rapport and a compassionate connection allow me to reality check with the participants, challenge them when they fall back to less effective positions and communications, and essentially promote a productive mediation process. In effect, I work cooperatively with the parties, guiding them in effectively communicating with each other so that they are properly prepared to search for options.

After Scarlett, Tamara, and their mothers told their uninterrupted stories, Heather and I began the process of having the girls speak directly with each other. As the repository of the conflict, we believed that it was more effective for the girls to talk with each other and to let the mothers observe. We coached, cajoled, challenged, supported, reframed, and persuaded them to communicate responsibly with each other. As this process unfolded, we found out that the girls had been pushed by their peers to escalate the conflict, and that neither really wanted to fight. In fact, before the peer group split, Scarlett and Tamara were best friends, and some of their anger toward each other was a reflection of their mutual hurt around losing the other's close friendship. Talking about this helped them understand and appreciate their common interest of attending high school and being in the local community without fear of retribution or attack. Both girls uncovered a common interest: living in a safe community environment.

As the conversation continued, the girls noticeably softened. This, in turn, led to the mothers' softening toward one another and toward their daughter's rival. Mutual misunderstanding was gradually replaced with a fragile but growing comprehension of the other's concerns. In addition, our effective use of humor, that is, humor that uncovered the irony of the situation rather than humor at the expense of one or both girls, reduced their seriousness and had the girls and mothers laughing together. We were ready to enter Stage IV.

Stage IV: Developing Options

Stage IV, "developing options," allows disputants the opportunity to brainstorm many possible solutions without fear of judgment. In their classic text, *Getting to Yes,* Harvard Negotiation Project authors Roger Fisher and William Ury (1991) say that brainstorming also encourages disputants to generate creative solutions and supports people in working "side-by-side." Brainstorming can be greeted initially with skepticism, since many people do not have experience with it. Moving the parties from sitting across from each other to sitting side-by-side can help. Physically facing a whiteboard or butcher block paper shifts the focus and the intention to help facilitate brainstorming.

From a Bowen theory perspective, I support the Stage III emphasis on brainstorming to generate options since this process also helps disputants to continue to let go of their rigid attachments to inflexible positions. In addition, brainstorming encourages the lightness of humor and laughter. By inventing outrageous ideas and then developing the most promising notions into realistic solutions, triangulation gets minimized as the conflict itself is removed from the emotional triangle and replaced by the most imaginative ideas from each party. As parties begin experiencing success with developing solutions and memorializing them in a written document, they begin to encounter the real possibility of working together cooperatively rather than fighting each other. This is especially important with participants who will maintain a relationship after the conflict is resolved. Even high-conflict people can learn to put aside preconceived notions about what the agreement should look like. In doing so, they can experience a glimmer of hope that successfully cooperating can achieve a positive result for all.

Brainstorming without judgment encourages outlandish thinking. Fisher and Ury suggest that creative possibilities are sometimes embedded in outrageous ideas and these potential solutions can be developed further. Other times, encouraging imaginative and crazy solutions gets people laughing, which is in itself beneficial to clear thinking and decreasing emotional reactivity.

Bowen theory suggests that cooperatively working side-by-side, decreasing emotional reactivity, connecting through laughter, encouraging thinking over reacting, and de-triangling the conflict from positional attachment to interest-based discussions are all important components for promoting increased functional differentiation in the moment. As functional differentiation increases, so, too, does the ability of the disputants to find long-term solutions to their intractable conflict.

By the time Scarlett and Tamara moved into Stage IV, while there was still tension between the two girls, there was also a developing atmosphere of cooperation and mutual understanding. We took out some butcher block paper and daughters and mothers brainstormed ways for the girls to avoid conflict and promote positivity in the future. A wild suggestion by Scarlett that her mother and she could move to Hawaii to avoid future conflict generated laughter. More thoughtful suggestions, such as the girls each speaking to their peer groups about staying out of their conflicts, were seed ideas that were later used to develop feasible agreements. As the participants become more comfortable with the brainstorming process, they become more confident about developing partial ideas into workable agreements.

Stage V: Writing the Agreement

When mediation reaches this stage, the parties are usually ready to finalize their agreements. By now, the most productive options generated in Stage IV have been refined by the parties and the mediator. At this point, the mediator's central task is to help the disputants clarify their thinking and translate the working agreement into B SMART language, which is a language familiar to most mediators. That is, the mediator helps the parties construct a plan that is *B*alanced, *S*pecific, *M*easurable, *A*chievable, *R*ealistic, and *T*imed.

Traditionally, Stage V crystallizes the participants' ideas into a written, practical document. From a Bowen theory perspective, I believe that agreement writing that is B SMART also helps create and maintain the conditions whereby clarity is maximized and misinterpretations are minimized. To this end, it is always better to have an agreement that is too specific rather than one that is not specific enough. While I remind the parties that they can jointly agree to change or modify aspects of the agreement, even if it becomes a court order, I inform them that the value of an unambiguous, articulate document is to provide clarity if, at a future time, emotionality runs high and clear-headedness becomes the first casualty of increased reactivity.

Writing B SMART agreements promote self-confidence for the disputants, as they realize that they are crafting an agreement of their own choosing and not relinquishing their personal responsibility and power to a judge or other authority figure. Since judges, by necessity of their time constraints, must make decisions quickly, most judges prefer that the parties in mediation be proactive and create their own agreements. Judges understand that the parties are often better equipped to create an agreement that meets the needs of their unique situation and that these agreements are more likely to stand the test of time.

Committing their cooperative agreement to a written document also encourages confidence between the participants. It is easier to believe that the other party will follow through with an agreement if both participants were actively involved in drafting it. Parties experience success as they learn to compromise, seek common and shared interests, and navigate conflicting interests in creating a workable agreement. This is especially important with medium-conflict and high-conflict parties, as writing a fair, balanced agreement helps promote a climate of trust, good will, and hope for the future.

From a Bowen theory perspective, agreements that are B SMART promote foresight, planning, clear thinking, and long-term outcomes, all functional processes of the prefrontal cortex. As participants move from emotional reactivity to clearheaded thinking, they are better able to self-regulate themselves and bring out the best in themselves and others.

Scarlett and Tamara, with the assistance of the co-mediators and mothers, crafted a fine agreement, which included, among other things, an agreement to not call each other's homes, apologies to the other parents for leaving obscene messages on their answering machines, an agreement to attempt to reconcile the split between the peer groups, and other mature decisions that indicated a willingness to move ahead with their lives and create the safety they both wanted and needed to be successful at school and in their communities.

Stage VI: Closing

If a written agreement is reached, the final stage of mediation is structured to congratulate the parties on their success. Copies of the agreement are distributed to each participant, and they are encouraged to begin implementing the plan in good faith, even before it becomes an order of the court (if the dispute is a part of the legal system). Participants, having successfully negotiated a mediation agreement based on common interests, have experienced something truly empowering. Even with disputants who enter mediation cautiously, suspiciously, and firmly entrenched in their positions, success in mediation can be transformative, thus shifting the emotional field of the participants and improving functional differentiation. Having been altered by the experience, they are better prepared for the future and their lives will be positively affected.

Even with partial agreements, participants can experience some success in negotiating agreements. Partial agreements provide an experience of cooperation and understanding between the parties, and this can set the tone for further cooperation and success, especially if the participants will be involved with each other in the future.

As a Bowen theorist mediator, I support all experiences of achievement, acknowledging the parties for their efforts, whether they reached a complete or a partial agreement. Reinforcing efforts to increase functional differentiation, while seemingly temporary, can offer the participants a positive experience of accomplishment and a glimpse into the world of the possible. After weeks or months of entrenched conflict or temporary emotional dislocation, a successful mediation can aid the parties in committing to a path of more mature decision making. Even when an agreement is not reached in mediation, I thank the participants for their good work and effort, acknowledging that these are difficult issues. I never take sides or blames one or both parties.

After we congratulated Scarlett, Tamara, and their mothers for their concerted efforts in fashioning a successful agreement, unexpectedly, the mothers decided to go to lunch together and the girls readily agreed! One of the joys of mediation is that we continue to experience those unexpected and rewarding surprises in our work. This was one such remarkable moment.

At its best, mediation is a transformative experience, helping parties to resolve a deep and troubling dispute and more confidently face the future. These emotional field shifts are not uncommon. In fact, using Bowen theory as a guide for mediations, emotional field shifts that increase functional differentiation occur regularly with participants, regardless of their socioeconomic status, race, ethnicity, religion, or education level. These shifts occur when parties are ready and willing to focus on finding common interests and take personal responsibility for their being and destiny.

While increasing basic differentiation provides a longer-term strategy for managing stress and uncertainty, participants who are willing to increase their responsible behavior in mediation and find new ways to connect with former adversaries are offered a glimpse of what is possible when they learn skills of self-management, calming down to think more clearly, and developing compassion for others. As such, even temporary increases in functional differentiation can illuminate a path toward more responsible and effective living.

Shifts in the emotional field that increase functional differentiation most commonly occur when the Bowen theorist practitioner remains a non-anxious presence in the mediation, clearly explains and promotes the process of mediation, relies on the stages of mediation as a guide rather than trying to will change through the force of personality and charisma, and intently guides the process without being attached to the form of the outcome. Even when participants cannot escape the swirl of emotional reactivity with one another and fail to reach an agreement, it is possible that the emotional maturity of the mediator may spark a flicker of hope and insight about a different way of thinking and behaving in the future.

Accessing Bowen theory as a guide is not a guarantee for conducting successful mediations. Mediators work with people operating at different levels of differentiation. Even capable, more mature parties can appear less adaptive and competent under the stress and turmoil of the conflict and disagreement. Those with less emotional resources and ability will likely go through the court system with higher levels of conflict, greater triangulation characterized by anxiety binding with their conflict, elevated emotional intensity, and less capacity to work responsibly and thoughtfully.

Not everyone is a candidate for mediation. High-conflict, extremely low-functioning parties may need the authority figure of the judge to tell them how to resolve their disagreement. The reality, of course, is there are no guarantees that even a judge's court order will ensure the end of the conflict. Some parties are so attached to their conflicts that they spend years emotionally entwined with each other through the conflict, incapable and unwilling to move forward with their lives. This kind of emotional fusion is regressive for both parties.

Nonetheless, Bowen theory provides an important framework for mediators. As applied in family therapy, education, business consulting, couples therapy, and other human systems forums, the Bowen theorist's focus is always on self-awareness, self-definition, and self-responsibility, as well as forging non-anxious connections with significant others in work and family environments. These same attributes and behaviors are equally effective in conducting mediations.

As a Bowen theorist and mediator, I find the theory a useful guide for my personal life and in my mediation work. The theory provides structure and direction. It allows me to monitor my responses and reactions. I am called to self-define and clarify my expectations in the mediation process. Applying Bowen theory requires me to manage my own emotionality so as to be effective in my work and in my own life. Bowen theory cautions me against activating the demons of willfulness in intense emotional environments. And it prods me to have fun with my work, to reach out compassionately to others in pain, and to respect disputants as people who are capable of managing their own lives. Bowen theory guides me in providing the necessary structure and safety to help disputants begin or continue the process of healing their conflicts and their lives.

Certainly, there are many effective mediators who are not Bowen theorists and who are not familiar with Bowen family systems theory. My observation of superior mediators, however, is that they utilize many of the principles of Bowen theory, even if they do not formally know the theory itself. Effective mediators, for example, know that disputants are more productive and effective when the mediator is calm and thus the environment is calm, when children are taken out of the middle of the conflict in domestic disputes, when processes and stages are followed, when rigid attachments to positions can be replaced by flexibly examining interests, when disputants are respected enough to develop and write their own agreements, when will conflicts are avoided with disputants, and when they can enjoy themselves by appreciating the diversity of people and the uniqueness of situations. All effective mediators remain fresh in their work by taking personal responsibility for their lives and by maintaining curiosity about what makes people tick.

All mediators are prone to errors in their work. The next chapter examines some common errors made by mediators and how applying the principles of Bowen theory can help reduce them.

Chapter Four

Common Errors and How Bowen Theory Can Minimize Them

This chapter investigates some common errors in mediation by mediators and how Bowen theory can help minimize their occurrence. Most mistakes by mediators reflect their own struggles with emotional maturity, anxiety, and reactivity. When levels of chronic and acute anxiety escalate, less well-differentiated mediators reflexively react with habitual and automatic thinking, feeling, and actions. They either over-function or under-function in their roles and responsibilities; they lose their capacity for resiliency and adaptability; they engage in will conflicts with the parties or the co-mediator; or they act in other ways that decrease the effectiveness of the mediation. After describing some common errors made by mediators, I will re-conceptualize the errors through Bowen theory and provide alternative ways of functioning that reflect more differentiated responses.

FAILURE TO ARTICULATE & FOLLOW THE STAGES: WHAT IS IT WE REALLY MEAN WHEN WE SAY, "TRUST THE PROCESS"?

Mediation can be conceptualized on a continuum from an informal to a formal process. Christopher Moore (1996), in his seminal book *The Mediation Process*, describes the range of variations on mediator roles and mediation procedures on a continuum "from highly directive to highly nondirective with respect to substantive issues, the problem-solving process, and the management of relationships between the parties" (p. 54). While there are varying perspectives about the function of the mediator and format of the mediation process, one of the most common mediation models is stage specific. Whether articulated as a five-stage approach, a six-stage process, or some other modification on the basic stages, most current mediation models rely on clearly articulated stages to train mediators, establish an effective foundation on which to conduct mediations, and provide guidelines for best practices.

Effective mediators rely on stages to frame the mediation, thus clarifying the mediation process through the stages and educating disputants about what to expect. Outlining and clarifying the mediation stages provide a safe crucible for transforming the parties' conflict and help ensure that everyone understands the roles of the disputants, the mediators, and the mediation itself. Clarity helps to diminish anxiety; clearness about the stages and the mediation process also assists with establishing a solid working foundation to promote effective conflict resolution.

More differentiated mediators also understand that the stages do not offer certainty of outcome and that the map is not the territory. That is, they recognize that, in practice, application of the stages is at best a fluid procedure. Rigid adherence to the stages does not allow flexibility for the unique circumstances of each mediation and can actually undercut the work of the parties and the mediator. Viewing the stages as a guide, then, rather than as an unalterable template demonstrates the mediator's emotional maturity through adaptability and flexibility in meeting the needs of the parties.

On the other end of the differentiation continuum, more poorly differentiated mediators either slavishly hold to implementing the stages, usually in an effort to diminish their own anxiety, or they ignore the stages in an effort to either impose their will on the disputants or because they believe that a more free-wheeling approach to mediation works best. In rigidly adhering to the stages, some mediators seek certainty and, out of personal discomfort, operate as if the map *were* the territory. That is, they believe that rather than the stages framing the discussion of the conflict, the stages are more important than the parties or the conflict itself. These mediators hold tightly to the stages and seek reduction of anxiety through adherence to the stages. Paradoxically, this rigidity undercuts the people and the process, and so diminishes the likelihood of an effective mediation.

On the other end of the anxiety-activated continuum, in conducting mediations too informally, these mediators minimize the importance of the stages and the structure it offers. Such mediators tend to be more emotionally immature, and they believe that convening the mediation itself provides the necessary and sufficient conditions for success. Often, these less differentiated mediators rely on willing change on the parties through sheer force of their personality, their charisma, or even their "expert" status. When the personality of the mediator becomes more important than the mediation process or the parties, mediator effectiveness diminishes. These mediators may impose agreements on the disputants through cajoling, bullying, lecturing, charming, and otherwise influencing the parties as "experts," but these agreements tend to be based on compliance or coercion rather than on promoting the personal responsibility of the parties. This approach undercuts the first and foremost ethical premise of mediation: self-determination by the parties involved in the conflict. Unfortunately, when agreements are the driving goal of mediation and become the need of the mediator rather than a goal for the disputants, agreements are less likely to withstand the test of time.

All of these reactions by mediators can also reflect inexperience or acute anxiety, rather than chronic anxiety and lower levels of basic differentiation. More highly differentiated but inexperienced mediators can suffer significant acute anxiety that fosters less effective practice. With mediator trainees and interns, more experience and successful supervision will promote best practices and their ineffectual behavior will likely decrease over time. With proper mentoring by more mature and seasoned mediators, less experienced mediators rapidly improve. If reactive and controlling behaviors by the mediator trainees and interns persist, however, these actions are more likely reflections of chronic anxiety and poorer levels of differentiation.

In summary, if mediators clearly articulate the stages of mediation in their introductions and understand that the stages act as a guideline rather than a grail, the stages can provide a structure within which to function, without unduly restricting the mediator and the disputants. When mediators say, "trust the process," that process is best understood as implementing the stages, which function as an anchor to return to, again and again, when conflict in mediation threatens to spiral out of control or when impasses seem unsolvable. That anchor provides a point of stability and focus for the mediator to help her manage her own emotional reactivity in turbulent waters.

NEUTRALITY, OBJECTIVITY, IMPARTIALITY, AND BALANCE

In traditional mediation training and literature, mediators are encouraged to develop and hone a sense of neutrality (Boulle, 1996; Folberg J and Taylor A, 1984). Neutrality is conceptualized as a state of mind and practice whereby mediators are non-judgmental of disputes and disputants, neither favoring one circumstance nor person over another. Many view mediator neutrality as offering the best possibility for effectively resolving conflict. Recently, the literature has been ripe with articles and chapters challenging the traditional notion of neutrality. Some wonder whether or not neutrality is even possible. Others suggest that neutrality may not even be desirable (Astor, 2007; Astor and Chinkin, 1992; Cohen, O, Dattner, N. and Luxenburg, A., 2007; Field,

2000; Mulcahy, 2001). Kathy McCormick (2009), who heads the Alternative Dispute Resolution Program through the Yavapai County Superior Court of Arizona, suggests that balance is more attainable and is more easily operationalized in mediation than neutrality. Rachael Field (2000) suggests that mediators replace the notion of neutrality with impartiality, which she defines as objectivity, fairness, and equitability. This is similar to McCormick's proposal regarding balance.

These authors and practitioners are wise to question the usefulness of promoting neutrality. When conceptualized as an either/or phenomenon, neutrality will inevitably fall short. That is, if the standard is whether or not a mediator is neutral or can act with absolute neutrality, the argument about the limited or even non-constructive value of neutrality holds sway. From a Bowen theory perspective, however, neutrality is re-conceptualized as objectivity. Michael Kerr and Murray Bowen (1988) define objectivity as the degree to which our thinking, feelings, and actions are not influenced by emotional reactivity and chronic anxiety. This definition more clearly approximates Field's (2000) notion of impartiality.

Objectivity and subjectivity exist on a continuum and are related to one's level of differentiation and thus chronic anxiety. In other words, the higher the level of differentiation, the lower the level of chronic anxiety and the more a person can think and act in a clearheaded manner, relatively unencumbered by automatic processes manifested by reactive thinking, feeling, and actions. The more emotionally mature person, then, has a greater capacity for passionate non-attachment. She can be fully engaged in the process, remain curious about the human condition, promote the effective functioning of the disputants, and remain relatively emotionally detached regarding the outcome of the mediation. A more emotionally mature mediator accepts responsibility for her functioning and performance in the mediation and allows the disputants to reach agreements, or not reach agreements, based on their own needs and wants. Conversely, the lower a person's level of differentiation, the higher the level of chronic anxiety, and the less capable he is of clearheaded, autonomous thinking and acting. As a consequence, this person is reacting more emotionally in the intellectual and feeling systems, resulting in actions that are driven more by anxiety and thus subjectivity than by calm focus, intentionality, and hence objectivity. These mediators are less balanced and impartial, and they are often attached to certain outcomes in mediation. For example, they may unduly pressure solutions on the parties, reject suggestions offered, do too much, or do too little. In these instances, the mediators operate with a higher level of subjectivity, and they undermine the mediation and mediation process.

From a Bowen theory perspective then, neutrality or objectivity is a *relative not absolute* concept, and is achieved more easily as differentiation increases and less easily as differentiation decreases. And, like differentiation itself, even those at the higher end of this 0 to 100 theoretical scale of differentiation rarely rise past 65 or 70, meaning that even those capable of greater objectivity and neutrality will react more subjectively a fair amount of time, especially as personal stress or intense conflict in the mediation rises. As a result, from a Bowen theory perspective, rather than discard the concept of neutrality entirely, we can use this important notion as a guide to increase our awareness of those persons and situations that cause us to reflexively and mindlessly react, so that we can maintain our commitment to promoting our own and others more thoughtful and autonomous thinking, feeling, and actions. For a Bowen theorist and practitioner, neutrality becomes a useful construct for measuring our personal capacity for passionate non-attachment and for deepening our obligation to personal responsibility, compassion, and self-regulation. The goal becomes increasing our level of neutrality or objectivity as a way of promoting effective conflict resolution.

McCormick's (2009) focus on balance is one technique for furthering this development. She believes that the more mediators are cognizant of maintaining balance in mediation, through alternating who gets to speak when, writing B SMART agreements, monitoring mediator responses for equity and consistency, etc., the greater the likelihood that the mediators will promote qualities associated with neutrality. Finally, neutrality should not be confused with lacking values or ethics. For example, if there is a power imbalance in mediation such that one party intimidates the other, or if the intimidating party threatens the mediator, the mediator may be forced to re-balance the mediation through caucus, strengthening his hand through greater control of the mediation process, or even ending the mediation itself. Neutrality does not mean abdicating responsibility for the mediation; rather, neutrality and objectivity require mediators to act in the best interest of the mediation and participants, protect the self, and continue to develop personal responsibility for one's thinking, feelings, and actions.

FAILURE TO READ ALOUD THE CONSENT DOCUMENT

One of the most common practices that I witness with co-mediators is the failure to read the consent document. When I query co-mediators about this decision, most have plausible explanations, which include that they summarize the key points in the introduction, and so believe that reading the document itself is redundant. They respect the parties' ability to read the document themselves, and they are cognizant of time constraints. While these points are all well taken, I believe that the extra few minutes it takes to read the consent document itself is well worth the investment for a number of reasons, including:

- Some people arrive in such heightened states of agitation and fear that they may not hear and understand what the mediator is saying in the introduction. Focusing them on the consent document by reading it, with them following along, slows down the process, helps parties focus on the essential components to the agreement, and, as a result, may diminish anxiety.
- For some individuals, English may be a second language. As such, they may not fully understand or even be able to read the document. It seems unethical to have a disputant sign a document without the full consent obtained by reading the entire agreement to them and asking them if they have any questions about the agreement.
- Finally, some people, even those for whom English is a primary language, are functionally illiterate. Illiteracy is widespread in certain portions of our society and can be embarrassing for people. Many individuals will not admit to their illiteracy, so reading the document provides the full consent necessary before beginning the mediation.

Reading the consent agreement seems like such a simple task, especially since the benefits of reading the form seem significant relative to the time and effort this requires. Doing so demonstrates the kind of intentionality, compassion, and respect that is the hallmark of more emotionally mature mediators.

OVER-FUNCTIONING AND UNDER-FUNCTIONING AS SYMPTOMS OF EMOTIONAL REACTIVITY

All of us have characteristic ways that we deal with uncertainty, agitation, anxiety, and fear. Usually, we either over-function, doing too much in an effort to control our environment and those in it, or we under-function, doing too little as we retreat from a challenging situation or person/people.

In mediation, there are many circumstances which can activate these characteristic patterns. When the mediation is progressing smoothly, most mediators are capable of tracking the process, managing the tasks, connecting with the participants, and writing competent agreements. As conflict rises, disputants' reactivity increases or impasses harden, mediators must reflect on their own reactions to these increasingly difficult scenarios. Automatic reactions may include doing too much or doing too little. For mediators, doing too much may include charging ahead, attempting to control the disputants, engaging in will conflicts to get the parties to cooperate, offering too many suggestions, denying the participants' intense feelings because of difficulties managing their own powerful feelings, and other behaviors that demonstrate disrespect for the disputants. Like any human system, when one person over-functions out of anxiety, the other person often under-functions, thus under-cutting his autonomous capacity. If a more mature disputant challenges the mediator's attempt at controlling the parties and the outcome, the mediation is likely to break down. In fact, this may be the healthiest response to an over-functioning mediator, since the over-functioner is not permitted to undercut the participant's competence.

One way more poorly differentiated mediators over-function is through the sheer force of their charismatic personalities. Relying on charisma can also have negative consequences in mediation. Friedman (1985) notes that char-ismatic leadership may initially prove useful for promoting group cohesion and effectiveness, but, over time, charismatic leaders tend to disempower groups, decrease maturity levels of its members, and increase the overall level of anxiety in a system. This is the same with disputants in mediation. If the parties rely too heavily on the mediator for suggestions, judgment, and approval, participants are inclined to under-function and agreements tend to be less favorable and less B SMART.

Under-functioning mediators are just as likely to undercut successful con-flict resolution. They may freeze up, do too little, defer to the co-mediator, or in other ways become less than fully present in the mediation. Their lack of "solid self" destabilizes the mediation process, and, unless the co-mediator can effectively step in and assume leadership, the mediation will likely fall apart. If no one holds the center, the disputants' conflict will likely escalate, and the parties will leave the mediation having suffered from the mediator's incompetence.

In both scenarios, the mediation and the profession suffer, and the parties lose the opportunity for resolving their own conflict. A mediator must culti-vate the qualities of personal reflection, self-management, intentionality, com-passion, respect, and personal responsibility in order to provide the best oppor-tunity for the disputants to find their own solutions. Proper mentor supervision or peer supervision can provide the guidance necessary for motivated trainees, interns, or mediators to change their automatic, emotional reactivity into more thoughtful, mindful, and autonomous responses. Changing ingrained patterns is never easy, though change is possible with the proper commitment, perse-verance, and willingness to honestly self-assess. And, a prolonged effort, over years and decades, to increase one's level of basic differentiation has universal benefits for work, friends, and family relationships. The payoff can be signifi-cant and meaningful. I will explore the importance of the mediator's emotional maturity and its effect on mediation in the next chapter.

Chapter Five

Emotional Maturity and the Mediator

This chapter explores the importance of the mediator's level of differentiation, or emotional maturity, as it relates to the success of the mediation process. I will examine the mediator and mediator team with regard to effective functioning within an executive leadership system. Further, I will consider the influence of the emotional field on the leadership system relative to the disputants and mediation.

This chapter is challenging to write. In suggesting that more highly differentiated mediators are more effective in work and in life, how do I avoid the corollary assumption that in order to write this chapter, I must be one of those mediators? Is it not presumptively arrogant of me to make such an assumption? Similarly, is it judgmental and haughty to assume that those with lower levels of basic differentiation are less effective in the world, especially when one of the premises of Bowen theory is that it describes rather than evaluates and so it is essentially non-judgmental? Can I accurately observe emotional maturity levels in my co-mediators since basic differentiation levels are best estimated over years and across a variety of circumstances?

These are questions I struggle with regularly. Nonetheless, as I age, a few observations and facts remain consistent. As described in the *Preface* of this book, I have been emotionally and intellectually captivated by Bowen theory since I was first immersed in it when Ed Friedman came to United States International University in 1986. This began my long-term relationship with the theory and its application. Since that time, I have applied the theory in many professional and personal relationships, from teaching to friendships, from administrative leadership to marriage, and from practicing as a family psychologist, mediator, and conciliator to fatherhood. I believe that with decades of commitment and effort, and with the advantage of professional colleagues and a loving wife familiar with Bowen theory and dedicated to their own professional and personal development, I am becoming more aware of both my strengths and my limitations. And, I observe incremental and cumulative changes in myself over the decades. As with many of us in mid-career and mid-life, I recognize that the fire that burns in mature adulthood is more steady and constant, whereas the fire that burns in youth and young adulthood is more erratic, inconsistent, and, sometimes, more dangerous. Self-confidence and personal acceptance increase with age, at least for those who believe that self-reflection and personal responsibility are important components of successfully aging.

If there is a lesson for me here, it is that I am more aware of my continuing proclivities for becoming anxious and reactive in certain situations, I am better (but by no means perfect!) at managing my chronic anxiety and emotional reactivity, and I have more acceptance of all parts of myself. Further, I have met many people in my life, including those whom I count as mentors, teachers, and guides. Some are further along the path of emotionally maturing, and, while I seek to emulate their compassion and wisdom, I try not to judge myself for not being more like them. Also, after decades of dedication, practice, and application, I believe that I can more accurately see systems and thus emotional reactivity and emotional immaturity in myself as well as others. Finally, one can intellectually understand and appreciate Bowen theory without embodying the theory. So, *in theory*, I can offer my observations about differentiation without concerning myself or the reader too much about how I fit into that equation!

Nonetheless, while I don't espouse any particular level of differentiation (Bowen claimed that we are too close to ever accurately assess ourselves in this way), I count myself fortunate for the opportunities that I have had and continue to have to differentiate. So, this chapter explores some of what I have learned along the way about differentiation and mediation.

THE EXECUTIVE SUBSYSTEM

Bowen theory, as well as other management theories and approaches, emphasizes the central importance of the executive subsystem for effective functioning (Bowen, 2002; Friedman, 1996; Goleman, D., Boyatzis, R. and McKee, A., 2002). Simply put, leadership begins at the top. Bowen theory views hierarchy as "written" into nature, espousing the significance of established hierarchy in the non-human world as a basic framework for the functioning of many mammalian and non-mammalian species (Ferrera, 1996). Hierarchy establishes a calm ordering in animal groups and provides protection for all members of the troop, hive, or pride. The functioning of the top member (or members) of the hierarchy is viewed as providing an emotional field or atmosphere that affects the entire system (Friedman, 1991; Goleman, D., Boyatzis, R. and McKee, A., 2002). This executive subsystem is, in effect, the primary determinant of the functioning of the entire system.

In human systems, this leadership phenomenon is observable in business, education, government, and families. In business, for example, consultant Jeffrey Miller (2002) observes that the maturity and integrity of the CEO sets the emotional tone for the rest of the company or organization. A more highly mature CEO is better able to provide clarity of mission, self-definition, and organizational vision. In addition, Bowen (2002) suggests that this person will provide continuous opportunities for those under her to promote their own differentiated functioning. In sum, the more emotionally mature leader emanates a more resonant emotional field or atmosphere in which all members of the organization can better perform. She neither over-functions, thus undercutting the performance and behaviors of subordinates, nor under-functions, hence increasing the stress on other workers to do more in order to pick up her pieces. The more differentiated leader, therefore, significantly influences and promotes better functioning in her followers (Bowen, 2002).

This phenomenon is observed in other human systems as well. Emotional intelligence writer and researcher Robert Boyatzis (2002) observes that the teacher providing more differentiated leadership to the classroom increases the functioning of her students. Parents, as the leaders of the family, set the emotional tone for their children (Kerr & Bowen, 1988). More poorly differentiated parents produce more anxious, under-functioning children. Better differentiated parents are able to create appropriate and intimate connections with their children, providing the best hope for raising more emotionally mature children and productive future citizens.

Similarly, from a Bowen theory perspective, mediation is conceptualized as a hierarchical system, with the mediator or the co-mediation team functioning as the executive subsystem. This does not mean that the mediator's role is more important than that of the disputants. Rather, it simply indicates that it is the mediator's responsibility to manage the process of mediation without controlling the disputants. For example, the mediator sets the emotional atmosphere for the mediation, establishes guidelines and ground rules, clarifies roles and expectations, clearly articulates the stages of mediation, and describes how they will be executed. In this way, by providing the "container" for mediation, the mediator establishes resonant leadership for the mediation system.

THE MEDIATOR'S LEVEL OF DIFFERENTIATION

Although the differentiation level of the disputants is important to the success of mediation, from a Bowen theory perspective, the mediator's basic level of differentiation is the single most relevant variable in securing a successful mediation. More highly differentiated mediators are more capable of responding to a variety of situations and conflicts. They are not attached to certain outcomes in the mediation. Rather, they can function admirably well in highly charged situations and can tolerate elevated levels of ambiguity and uncertainty. Although not attached to outcomes, these mediators are fully involved in the process, staying connected to all parties throughout the mediation. They clearly outline the expectations, structure, and roles of all involved; are self-defined and thus manage the mediation process without controlling the parties or the outcome; and use appropriate humor to lighten the emotional atmosphere and de-escalate the seriousness that highly invested people bring to the negotiating table.

While more highly differentiated mediators may find themselves more attentive to one of the disputants or more connected to one proposed solution over another, they are capable of remaining fairly neutral, balanced, and objective. Like coaches for a team, they help bring out the best in the "players" without getting on the field and playing themselves. They neither over-function nor under-function out of anxiety. That is, they create an environment where all of the parties can fully and appropriately participate in their respective roles. They fully engage with disputants without being demanding. They understand the importance of creating a crucible for change without being invested in outcome.

In contrast, less emotionally mature mediators see themselves as directors and players rather than as coaches. They are often attached to outcomes and become triangulated in the conflict by siding with one individual or group over the other, or they push their own agendas for a solution and agreement. They are more emotionally anxious and react from subjective positions that are usually not in the best interests of the mediation process. Less differentiated mediators do not tolerate highly charged situations well. They seek certainty and control and are uncomfortable in ambiguous environments. Often, they engage in unproductive conflicts of will with disputants in an effort to get them to change or agree to a particular outcome. Rather than releasing into the process, they may experience anxiety, anger, frustration, and other feelings that emotionally undermine the mediation. Heightened chronic anxiety can drive a mediator to over-function, assuming too active and directive a role.

An over-functioning mediator may, in turn, influence the disputants to under-function and not take full responsibility for the mediation. Conversely, high levels of chronic anxiety may drive the mediator to under-function, resulting in the loss of perspective and neutrality, without which the parties cannot safely and fully explore the issues and the conflict. Agreements facilitated by less differentiated mediators do not usually follow B SMART guidelines. These written agreements may not withstand the test of time. More often than not, mediation breaks down as one of the parties becomes aware of the non-neutrality and reactivity of the mediator.

In sum, the mediator's emotional maturity sets the tone for the mediation. The more he is able to personally engage the disputants, remain clear about the process of mediation, self-regulate in the intense emotional environment of mediation where conflict is high and has the potential to escalate rapidly, and provide leadership for the disputants without over-functioning, the greater the likelihood for a successful mediation.

While the differentiation level of the mediator is the most significant variable for mediation success, it is not the only critical variable. The other vital factor is the differentiation level of the disputants. Notably, even a more differentiated mediator can be relatively ineffective in an escalating system of conflict and blame. Nonetheless, if the mediator can "hold the center," that is, maintain his calm in turbulent waters, and remain a part of the process without becoming part of the conflict, mediation has a significantly higher likelihood of succeeding.

I describe this state of equilibrium as *passionate non-attachment*. The mediator is most effective when she is fully engaged in the process without being attached to the form of the outcome or any particular outcome itself. Bowen theorist and business consultant Kathleen Wiseman (1996) describes this process as going to the bleachers, and William Ury (1993) refers to this concept as going to the balcony. Bowen theorists conceptualize the importance of increased emotional separation from the intense emotional field as critical to maintain relative objectivity within the system.

From a practical point of view, the responsibility of the mediator, then, is to know his strengths and weaknesses, understand what issues are personally challenging, and develop strategies for self-regulation when the limbic brain's fight-flight activation occurs. All individuals, including mediators, bring personal histories to their work. For example, a mediator may relate too closely to the challenges or the profile of a disputant and subsequently find it a struggle to maintain balance, neutrality, and relative objectivity. Adherents of Bowen family systems theory do not suggest that only highly differentiated people can function well in leadership positions. These types of struggles are common to all leaders. That said, the mediator, as the executive leader of the process, must develop an awareness of personal functioning and make a conscious commitment to self-examination before blaming a difficult or failed mediation on disputants. In asking disputants to assume personal responsibility, mediators must exemplify responsible behaviors themselves. Echoing regressive elements in society at large, it is often easier to blame another rather than honestly face personal shortcomings. More emotionally mature mediators avoid this pitfall.

A genuine willingness to take personal inventory of one's strengths and challenges is an important initial step. Beyond that, however, committed and highly effective mediators assume personal accountability. They examine their own lives with intentionality, mindfulness, and compassion, key qualities of those with increasing emotional maturity. This personal commitment, in turn, translates into a more resonant emotional field for their work. That is, they create an atmosphere conducive to conflict resolution, if not conflict transformation.

There are many techniques for improving self-regulation and decreasing emotional reactivity. These include meditation, neurofeedback, tai chi, prayer, reflection, regular exercise, psychotherapy, working with a Bowen theory coach, and a host of other personal practices. Many paths can help achieve the desired result of increasing self-differentiation and any path can fail as well. It is not the path itself that becomes the determining variable; rather, it is the focused mindfulness and long-term commitment to the approach that may be more important. Understanding systems and thinking systemically can lead to thinking, feeling, and acting differently. The key, it seems, is learning to maintain calm in an emotional storm. No one accomplishes this perfectly and, at best, most people are capable of this self-regulation perhaps about seventy percent of the time. The goal becomes increasing one's capacity for self-definition, self-regulation, and relationship connection, not the artificial and unattainable goal of accomplishing it perfectly all of the time. In essence, effective mediators cultivate a commitment to their own emotional development and maturity as they realize that who they are and what they bring to the mediation is of critical importance to the success of the mediation itself.

In addition to self-monitoring and self-regulating their own level of reactivity, there are other practical measures that mediators can take to improve their functioning. For example, mediators can schedule mediations at times when they are least stressed or at times of the day when they function best. Also, by becoming aware of their own emotional triggers, mediators can better serve their disputants. Mediators must know what they are comfortable managing and what creates noteworthy emotionality. Everyone has emotional triggers that negatively impact their effectiveness. Violence, threats, child abuse, and sexual exploitation can all invoke strong negative reactions in a mediator. Knowing her triggers allows a more reflective mediator to take steps to minimize adverse effects on the mediation process. For example, she can work with a co-mediator, decline the case, or seek supervision in situations that might prove emotionally challenging. Proactive and corrective behavior can only be initiated through self-knowledge, a hallmark of increased differentiation.

CO-MEDIATION AND EXECUTIVE SYSTEM FUNCTIONING

A co-mediation model is common. In some work environments, mediators select their co-mediators; in other contexts, co-mediators are more randomly paired. I work at a courthouse where co-mediation pairing is often random, so I have worked with co-mediators with a range of emotional maturity. Co-mediator pairings from different levels of emotional maturity create different challenges and rewards.

The functioning and effectiveness of the executive subsystem becomes more complicated with the introduction of the co-mediator team. While there are many possibilities regarding differentiation levels and the co-mediation team, I will address three important pairings. The first and most promising pairing is with co-mediators who have approximately the same, moderately high level of differentiation. The second pairing involves co-mediators at relatively different levels of basic differentiation, one is more highly differentiated and the other is more poorly differentiated. The third possibility is the pairing of co-mediators who have similar levels of moderately low differentiation.

The first scenario is optimal, i.e., two relatively differentiated mediators working together. Both are mature enough to work cooperatively, support one another in the mediation, and thus promote the effective functioning of the executive subsystem. They fully engage with the disputants, commit to the mediation process, relax into their work, and use effective humor to help calm the emotional intensity that the disputants bring to mediation. These co-mediators remain clear, solid, and active members of the mediation system. Their work together has a natural flow so that each takes turn leading and following, with neither mediator over-functioning or under-functioning in the executive system or with the disputants themselves. Both naturally trust and support each other, easily reinforce important statements by the other, and continuously develop and express a unified voice to the participants. In effect, the emotional tone or atmosphere created and perpetuated by the team is one of resonant cooperation, hope, engagement, and enjoyment, with neither attached to a particular outcome. They rarely get caught by the anxiety of the parties or the situation and tend to work in fluid synchrony. While each may, from time to time, become reactive to a particular disputant or conflict situation, each possesses enough self-awareness and self-responsibility to acknowledge this anxiety and address it with the co-mediator. The co-mediating partner can then take the lead or can at least help the mediator monitor his functioning during these times. There is enough trust and support in the team so that they, in effect, present a "united front" to the disputants, each occupying the same point in the mediation triangle.

This circumstance of essentially equal and moderately high co-mediator differentiation is less about the skill level of the mediators than it is about emotional maturity, personal integrity, and a willingness to live an examined life and grow one's own level of differentiation to increase effectiveness as a person and as a mediator. It behooves all mediators to cultivate these effective co-mediator relationships, as they have the capacity to "imprint" the potential for success on the disputants. That is, the higher the emotional maturity of the co-mediation team, the greater the probability for a successful mediation, as a positive emotional resonance saturates the encounter (Goleman, D., Boyatzis, R. and McKee, A., 2002).

Working with these co-mediators is one of the great pleasures in conducting mediations, and I am fortunate to count several co-mediators at the courthouse in this category. They embody the principles of differentiated leadership in the mediation environment. They understand the value of meeting beforehand to discuss the case and our roles in it, and we discuss anything unusual about the upcoming mediation or anything that might personally affect our participation that day. There is a natural give and take in the sessions themselves, with each co-mediator leading and following as the situation demands. These co-mediators and I remain flexible with each other and with the parties, while remaining committed to containing the participants in a safe and supportive emotional and structural environment. Each mediation is approached with fresh eyes and an openness to learn from the encounter. Mediations that produce B SMART agreements are celebrated, while those that do not result in agreements are reviewed afterwards with an eye toward learning from the encounter. Perhaps just as importantly, these co-mediators and I enjoy working together and have fun with our work. Using Bowen theory as a guide, these co-mediators are committed to professional excellence and personal maturity. I have ascertained from experience which co-mediators are highly functioning and conducting mediations with those partners is enjoyable and productive.

In the second scenario, one mediator exhibits a significantly higher level of differentiation than the co-mediator. In essence, the executive subsystem is imbalanced. One mediator contributes to the success of the mediation and one mediator undermines the mediation through emotional reactivity and non-productive participation. The less emotionally mature co-mediator is usually over-controlling, manipulative, and does not promote an emotionally and structurally safe environment for disputants. I know of one mediator, for example, who uses excessive self-disclosure in trying to "relate" to the disputants. The most mature disputants reject these awkward attempts. Unfortunately, most parties, being in vulnerable positions and seeking the guidance of the mediator to steer them through unfamiliar terrain, remain confused by these ineffective tactics. Less differentiated mediators create interlocking triangles that generate or amplify the chronic anxiety in the system, making it difficult for the more differentiated co-mediator to manage.

The less differentiated member finds it difficult to remain objective, balanced, and relatively neutral. She may over-function either in the co-mediation relationship or the mediation process itself. Manifestations of over-functioning might include talking too much or dominating the process through advice-giving, injecting a personal agenda, or providing other extraneous input. In effect, a less emotionally mature co-mediator experiences general challenges with one or more areas of self-regulation. This type of mediator does a disservice to the mediation process and to the field of mediation. Rather than being committed to the edict, "mediator know thyself," the less differentiated co-mediator plays out her immaturity in the mediation. The biggest challenge for the more highly differentiated co-mediator is to not get reactive to the reactivity of the co-mediator. Friedman (1991) says that one definition of differentiation is the ability to remain calm and engaged in the presence of pressure. If the more differentiated co-mediator can remain balanced, neutral, and appropriately active, the mediation may not be lost. There is even the possibility that the less differentiated mediator will calm down and function better as well. Goleman (2006) makes the point that calmness is contagious. This is the same principle that predicts that disputants will function better as a result of working with a more highly differentiated mediator. A system is a system whether the lens is focused on the co-mediator team or the disputants. Everyone benefits if even one mediator can remain non-reactive and appropriately involved with the process. Of course, the context of the mediation is the responsibility of the co-mediators, and it is they who must determine the best course of action. The ethical commitment must be to the mediation process and the disputants, providing them with the best opportunity for self-determination and a positive outcome.

The option of choosing a co-mediator varies in different circumstances. In private settings, most mediators have a voice in co-mediation selection. In these situations, there may be a natural tendency to select co-mediators at about the same level of differentiation. Bowen theory suggests that marriages work this way, with parties selecting each other at about the same degree of emotional maturity. Selecting a co-mediator in private settings may be influenced by the same automatic, "unconscious" factors. In other mediation settings, such as the courts and community mediation centers, co-mediators may be more randomly paired. In circumstances such as these, random pairings may result in an imbalance in the differentiation levels of the co-mediators. Having experienced this in my own work, I have developed a variety of useful strategies over the years for increasing the likelihood of mediation success.

For example, with all co-mediation teams, it is important for the co-mediators to spend time together before beginning the mediation. This allows the mediators to connect with each other, develop an initial strategy together (particularly if the mediators haven't worked together previously), and communicate important issues that might affect the mediation. Establishing a personal connection that allows for cooperation and fluency in the co-mediation relationship is always important. It is especially critical if there is an imbalance in differentiation levels between the mediators.

During the pre-mediation check-in, I ask to initiate the introduction phase, thus setting the terms of the mediation and providing the initial emotional imprint on the process. Beginning the mediation process by clearly articulating stages, defining roles, and establishing guidelines and procedures can have a calming effect on the disputants as well as on the less competent mediator. A well-executed introduction helps create a structure for positive, respectful dialogue throughout the mediation and promotes hope for a successful interaction between the disputants. I find that by emphasizing the importance of structure and process, I am not only educating disputants about the importance of creating a safe "container" for mediation, but also re-educating the less differentiated mediator about best practices.

For example, I once worked with a co-mediator, "Mark," who is known as an over-functioner who dominates mediations, is very casual about stages and processes, and whose mediations are known for their excessive length. Before our mediation commenced, I approached Mark and made a personal connection with him, consciously but subtly assuming the dominant leadership of the co-mediation system. I informed Mark about how the mediation would be conducted and our respective roles in the process. The art was to find a way to control the mediation process without engaging in a conflict of wills with Mark. By setting the terms for mediation during the introduction stage, Mark calmed down, and the disputants benefited from our cooperative working environment.

To the degree that it is ethically and practically possible, my task is to develop an effective working relationship with the less capable co-mediator for the sake of the mediation itself. As such, I find ways for the less differentiated co-mediator to "fill in," rather than having her lead. I make a conscious effort to reinforce positive statements when the co-mediator makes them. Basic reinforcement techniques can be helpful, i.e., positively reinforcing useful statements and minimizing problematic behaviors and statements by ignoring them. If the co-mediator makes particularly inappropriate or unhelpful comments, I try to reframe them in ways that better serve the co-mediation team and thus the mediation by detoxifying harsh comments to make them more positive or effective.

If a co-mediator is impeding the progress of the mediation, I might convene a caucus to discuss these issues. Finding ways to positively challenge the co-mediator can be difficult. Descriptive language rather than evaluative language works best. For example, an evaluative statement is: "Your incessant storytelling is driving me crazy and undercutting our work here." A descriptive statement is: "I find myself distracted with your stories and suggest we allow the parties more time to discuss the issues together." It can be difficult engaging in these confrontations. In these circumstances, it is important to remain as calm and as non-reactive as possible in an emotionally charged field made more confusing or conflictual by the less able mediator. At all times, I remind myself to stay focused on my work, to remain responsible for the mediation process, and to encourage the disputants to assume personal responsibility for resolving their conflict. In sum, I assume the central mediator role, while delegating a secondary or tertiary role to the co-mediator.

In general, the over-functioning of the more differentiated mediator is not an effective long-term strategy. Over-functioning is a part of a two-person reciprocal relationship that is imbalanced. Over-functioning by one person in a two-person relationship promotes under-functioning in the other person, just as under-functioning in a two-person relationship promotes over-functioning in the other party. Nonetheless, in working with a less emotionally mature co-mediator, over-functioning may protect the integrity of the mediation. It may, however, encourage unhealthy competition and increased conflict, thus undermining the disputants' self-determination. To circumvent this situation, I try to constructively engage with the less emotionally mature co-mediator by being personable, clear, direct, firm, and compassionate. Under no circumstance, however, will I compromise my personal integrity or the integrity of the mediation itself by allowing the less differentiated mediator to take over or undermine the mediation. In extreme instances, the more mature mediator can ask the less mature co-mediator to excuse herself from the mediation or suggest that they consult with a supervisor on how best to proceed. Fortunately, I have never found myself in such an extreme situation.

Of great concern is the possibility that the co-mediator differentiation imbalance can result in the disputants splitting the co-mediation team. Disputants may find themselves subtly pressured to support one mediator over the other, creating unproductive and interlocking triangles. In the ensuing power play, the needs of the disputants will become marginalized and tangential to the conflict between the mediators. Obviously, this kind of triangulation must be avoided at all costs. Sometimes, additional training helps less differentiated mediators. More often, though, the problematic behaviors need to be addressed through critical self-examination, the acceptance of personal responsibility, and honest scrutiny as to whose needs are being met by the mediation process. Only if the less differentiated mediator is willing to confront his personal challenges, unhelpful interjections, and misperceptions is there hope for constructive change. Unfortunately, those most needing this honest self-examination are often least willing to engage in it.

The third possibility is that the members of co-mediation team are at similar levels of moderately low differentiation. This circumstance is the most problematic. The lower the co-mediators' basic differentiation, the more chronic anxiety dominates the mediation process through higher levels of blaming, less resiliency, greater emotional reactivity, and more chaos. These mediators will have the most difficulty remaining neutral and de-triangled from the disputants' issues. More poorly differentiated co-mediators are less resilient and have less capacity to creatively respond to stressful material and situations. Their ability to function as an effective team is compromised by their low level of integrity and maturity.

It is always preferable for mediators to be more emotionally mature than their disputants. Mediators are the keepers of the process. Disputants look to them to guide the mediation, provide safety, develop good will with and between the participants, and manage the mediation in order to keep things safe and under control. In addition, while mediation follows a defined, though not rigid, format, there is usually a high level of ambiguity and uncertainty. Anything can and will happen and mediators must feel comfortable in these stressful environments. More highly differentiated people manage ambiguity well; some even thrive in environments that are uncertain, enjoying the creative potential. Less differentiated people seek certainty and find safety and comfort through control. Control tactics often take the form of *will conflicts*, which Friedman (1987) defines as attempts to force others to think, feel, and act in specifically defined ways. Unfortunately, will conflicts also undercut the functioning of the parties being willed and, so, should be avoided.

The best way to manage these problematic pairings is to avoid them. If more poorly differentiated mediators will not self-regulate themselves and assume greater personal responsibility, peer regulation and supervisor regulation becomes critical. As mediators, we are ultimately responsible for ensuring the integrity of the profession and the protection of the public. Peers must express their concerns directly to these problematic mediators and to their supervisors. Trainers and supervisors must take great care as gatekeepers of the profession, providing opportunities for trainees and interns to improve and, ultimately, not certifying those incapable of providing a quality service to others. Without this level of peer and supervisor responsibility and regulation, the profession will be compromised. With it, the profession will be strengthened and will continue to grow.

The most crucial variable for successful mediation is the emotional maturity level of the mediators because, according to Bowen theory, the leadership team of the mediator (or co-mediators) "emotionally imprints" the mediation process, thus affecting the likelihood for success or failure. If mediators, like all leaders in any human system, accept personal responsibility for their thinking, feelings, and actions through a willingness to live an examined life of mindfulness, intentionality and compassion, mediations will be more fun, more effective, and, ultimately, more successful.

The next chapter addresses the second-most important Bowen theory concept relevant to mediation, emotional triangles and their influence on mediation success.

Chapter Six

Emotional Triangles, Triangulation, and De-Triangulation in Mediation

Perhaps the most important Bowen theory concept is differentiation, as a person's differentiation level is the most significant determinant of adaptability, resiliency, emotionally mature responding, and even the probability of getting caught by a conflict to the point of needing mediation. Chronic anxiety is the reciprocal of differentiation and describes a person's inherited reactivity in the face of pressure and conflict (Kerr and Bowen, 1988).

Mediation involves people in stressful situations, and functional differentiation is impacted by stress. Bowen theory proposes that stress is managed automatically through creating emotional triangles and the binding of chronic anxiety. As such, an understanding of the relationship between differentiation, chronic anxiety, and emotional triangles is critical to comprehending and effectively conducting mediations. As discussed in Chapter 2, when any two-person system is under stress, a third person or third other (substance, money, belief, object, etc.) may be pulled in to reduce the stress, at least temporarily. This process binds anxiety in a two–person system, and it is called triangulation or being triangled. Triangulation is an automatic reaction to stress and is therefore universal. That is, everyone is prone to triangulate when a relationship is pressurized.

The higher a person's level of basic differentiation, the less she triangulates. Inversely, the more chronic anxiety and the less basic differentiation in a person, the more he triangulates. Without being able to "see systems" and the triangling process, the mediator will become the "third leg" of the stressed system. For a successful outcome, the mediator must avoid getting caught by the inherent anxiety of the mediation process. The higher differentiation level of the mediator enables her to keep calm and stay out of the emotional triangle, which greatly enhances the probability of an effective mediation.

As such, understanding the nature of emotional triangles and the process of de-triangulation are the most important "techniques" of Bowen theory applied to mediation. These techniques are really ways of thinking about processes that influence how one effectively manages oneself in a pressurized situation. Without the ability to appropriately self-regulate, the techniques will be ineffective. To successfully navigate the chronic anxiety and stress of the mediation environment, the mediator must understand the nature of emotional triangles and triangulation, consciously avoid getting emotionally triangulated into the disputants' conflict, and know how to extricate herself if and when triangulation occurs.

This constant, conscious focus on both internal and external processes (that is, understanding and managing both the individuality life force and the togetherness life force) is required to successfully navigate all important relationships. In mediation, understanding emotional triangles and these related concepts with a commitment to self-functioning is crucial for success. This chapter will investigate the application of emotional triangles, triangulation, and de-triangulation to mediation, beginning with the simplest mediation, the three-person mediation system, and moving through more complex mediations with additional participants, co-mediators, attorneys, and stakeholder groups.

THE SOLO MEDIATOR AND TWO DISPUTANTS: THE UNCOMPLICATED, CENTRAL TRIANGLE IN MEDIATION

As discussed in Chapter 2, "Understanding Bowen Theory," under stress, a two-person system will automatically bring in a third person or "other" to help create temporary stability (Kerr and Bowen, 1988). Disputants in mediation have triangulated the conflict or the issue into their dispute, thus binding their anxiety around the dispute. This can take the form of wages in business-labor mediations, old growth forests in environmental-developer mediations, faulty products in civil mediations, or custody of and access to children in domestic mediations. The degree of attachment or fusion to the "anxiety binder" and the level of the disputants' differentiation drive them to more or less reactive positions and escalating conflict. The goal of mediators is to help the parties de-triangulate the conflict. De-triangling the conflict means reducing the intensity and reactivity around the dispute. This, in turn, helps the parties move away from the rigidity of their calcified positions, allowing them to think more clearly, examine common interests, and come up with workable solutions.

To accomplish this end, a mediator must form, what I term, a *mediation triangle*. A mediation triangle is an attempt by the mediator to insert herself into the disputants' system by connecting equally with each party (similar to creating equidistant sides of an equilateral triangle). The connection must be as differentiated as possible. That is, the mediator must have a strong, non-anxious presence, clear boundaries, and a firm capacity for self-definition and self-regulation. In addition, she must develop strong rapport with the parties through compassion, understanding, and clarity about each person's roles and responsibilities in the mediation process. Through that more differentiated connection, it is possible to lessen the fusion that attaches the parties to the anxiety binder (i.e. dispute) by temporarily increasing the functional differentiation of the disputants in the mediation system. That is, as the disputants feel more connected to and trusting of the mediator, the emotional intensity around the dispute de-escalates and they begin focusing their attention on the mediator, rather than solely on the issue in conflict.

In a best-case scenario, the mediating triangle becomes, what I call, a *differentiating triangle*. I have developed the concept of the differentiating triangle as a counterpoint to the concept of triangulation (Regina, 2000). That is, in triangulation, two people in conflict deal with anxiety by bringing in a third to bind the anxiety for them. This reaction temporarily stabilizes the conflict and reduces short-term anxiety. The unfortunate result is that triangulation is a "false" solution, as it raises long-term anxiety and ultimately decreases functioning and adaptability.

An example of this is with Wynonna and Devon, a married couple that triangulated alcohol into their relationship. The alcohol-abusing Devon temporarily decreased anxiety within the marital system by reducing the pressure on the couple for intimacy. As can be expected, however, alcoholism brings with it the likelihood of seriously decreased functioning on the part of one or both of the spouses. Eventually, the marriage de-stabilized, Wynonna and Devon began divorce proceedings, and they participated in mediation to develop a parenting plan. Alcohol abuse and dependency became an anxiety binder for the couple, and the parents got stuck around parenting access due to Devon's drinking. Wynonna refused to allow unsupervised access to the children for Devon, despite the fact that he was often alone with the children when they were married. Instead of focusing on the best interests of the children—their safety and their access to both parents—Wynonna and Devon got hyper-fixated around their rigid positions of supervised vs. unsupervised access. Access, and the bound anxiety around this issue, became the emotional triangle, with each vying for the inside position with the children.

In contrast, a differentiating triangle is one in which three people or two people and a third "other" are connecting in such a way that creativity, problem solving, or other higher-level functioning or adaptation is possible. For example, two parents learn and grow from each other and their child in ways that help each other become more emotionally mature, which in turn strengthens the family and promotes differentiation in their daughter. As a second example, two composers can create a differentiating triangle such that together they write an exquisite piece of music. For Wynonna and Devon, creating a mediation triangle with me allowed them to focus on the best interests of their children, which was raising them in a *safe* and loving environment. Near the end of the mediation, as defenses were lowered and a semblance of trust re-established, a differentiating triangle developed between the three of us such that the parents were able to apologize for their years of secrets and lies. This, in turn, helped create a climate of mutual respect, benefiting the children and helping with the transition to a two-household family.

It is theoretically possible that a mediator, or mediator team, can bring such a highly differentiated presence to the mediation and thus shift the emotional field of the mediation system to a "higher" level of differentiation. I believe that the most effective mediators in the profession are capable of such emotional field shifts. In these situations, the parties report that the mediator "brought out the best in them." The parties may walk away not only with a solid agreement that holds over time but also with a true understanding of and respect for the other party. In this scenario, mediation itself can be a transformative experience. In the victim-offender mediation example described in Chapter 3, at the end of the mediation, Scarlett's and Tamara's mothers suggested that all four of them go out to lunch, to which the girls agreed. Heather and I, as co-mediators, viewed this development as a transformative experience for the parties that was facilitated by cultivating both a mediation triangle and a differentiating triangle. When these transformational moments occur, they are truly magical to witness.

When working solo, the mediator has the advantage of operating without the complications that sometimes accompany the co-mediation relationship. This is especially true with simple mediations involving two disputants. While these mediations can include all the hallmarks of more complicated mediations (emotional intensity and reactivity, high stakes outcomes for the parties, etc.), for the mediator, the mediation process itself is more clearly visible and easier to manage.

In mediations with a solo mediator and two disputants, the parties arrive in mediation with the central triangle clearly identified: each of the disputants and the conflict or issue itself occupies separate points on the triangle. In its simplest form, there are no other persons or variables involved in the conflict. This is called a *simple or uncomplicated emotional triangle*. In these instances, the parties are usually vying for the inside position of the triangle

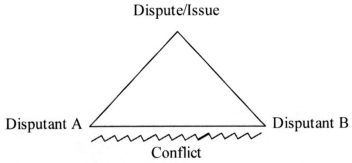

Figure 6.1.   Central, Uncomplicated Triangle.

with the conflict or issue. That is, each party wishes the dispute resolved in his or her way. The emotional triangle is thus a central triangle and an uncomplicated triangle.

For example, Roberto and José were cousins who entered mediation from small claims court over a $5,000 personal loan José made to Roberto. José wanted immediate repayment; Roberto said that he could repay the loan but he asked for a reduction in the loan principal and a generous long-term repayment schedule over an extended period of time. Depending on the differentiation level of the parties and the degree of anxiety binding the conflict, this mediation could have been pretty straightforward. As discussed in Chapter 3, "Applying Bowen Theory to the Six-Stage Process of Mediation," the mediator seeks to develop a mediation triangle through rapport and confidence building with both sides. This process occurs throughout the mediation, but it is particularly central to the first two mediation stages and the caucus. The mediator attempts to lessen the stranglehold of fusion that each brings to the mediation through rigid attachment to positions, anger about not being treated fairly by the other, and other emotionally reactive stances. As the mediator is able to lessen the anxiety of the system through empathy, humor, rapport, clarity of stage execution and role expectations, shifting from positions to interests, reframing, and compassion, the central triangle of their conflict begins to de-rigidify, unbind, and shift. This lessening of the attachment to the conflict or outcome situates the mediator to develop a mediation triangle, allowing the parties to more responsibly explore the conflict, search for options, and develop workable solutions.

The key danger is that the mediator will get "caught" by the anxiety of the system and become triangled into the conflict, thus becoming a part of the problem rather than a part of the solution. Of all the possible scenarios, however, the single mediator and two disputants remains the simplest of all mediation possibilities. Other possibilities present more challenges.

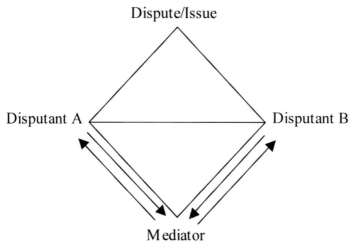

Figure 6.2. Development of a Mediation Triangle.

In this example, as the issues were explored, it became evident that rather than a simple triangle, Roberto and José were involved in possibly illegal activities, and the loan was a part of these activities. While the parties did not state that the loan was to finance the purchase and use of illegal substances, I understood the essence of this context through the parties' discussions. The central triangle was now a complicated triangle as other family members lined up with the parties to occupy points on the triangle. In this instance, cousins Roberto and José were involved in the undocumented loan transaction and their respective wives, Carlotta and Paula became their allies. The wives each occupied a point on the triangle with their husbands. This created a *complicated triangle*, which Kerr and Bowen (1988) define as a triangle with more than one person at one or more points. Complicated triangles further intensify emotionality, and solutions become more difficult to formulate.

As disputants, Roberto and José not only had to navigate their conflict with each other but they were also acutely aware of the positions of their respective wives. In general, as the number of involved parties increases or as the issue itself gets linked to other issues, the conflict between a two-person system is no longer contained between the two parties and the dispute or issue itself. Interlocking and complicated triangles form, thus increasing the complexity and difficulty of the mediation. In this example, threats of police involvement created an interlocking triangle between the disputants and the police or potential police action.

To review, the unpaid loan generated anxiety between the cousins, Roberto and José. This anxiety increased and then "spilled" out of the overloaded two-

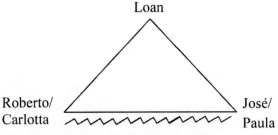

Figure 6.3.   Central, Complicated Triangle.

person system and created a central triangle, with money at the third point of the triangle. The anxiety in the central triangle was amplified by the spouses, Carlotta and Paula, who each felt that her husband was being unfairly treated by his cousin. The conflict escalated, with threats and counter-threats of police involvement generating more anxiety. This anxiety spiraled out of the central, complicated triangle and created an interlocking triangle between the disputants, their wives, and the threat of police involvement.

Navigating the complexity of interlocking triangles is dependent on the mediator's ability to stay focused on her own functioning, to be viewed as an expert, to develop rapport with the disputants, to cultivate a mediation triangle, to help them sort out the conflict, to shift from positions to interests, to generate options, to explore BATNAs and WATNAs, and to write B SMART agreements. By minimizing the anxiety that comes from complicated and interlocking triangles, and by focusing on the most salient issues of the conflict, solo mediators are usually successful in defusing the intensity of the conflict

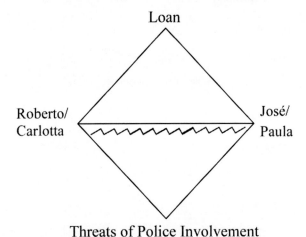

Figure 6.4.   Interlocking Triangle.

and helping the parties reach agreement. As the mediation triangle was firmly established through the stages of the mediation process, Roberto and José were ready to discuss their interests more rationally and clearly. Family was important to them and, as cousins, they did not want money to permanently harm their relationship. Money had been successfully de-triangled from their relationship and, with my assistance, they were able to formulate an acceptable repayment plan.

The issues become more complex, however, with more mediation participants.

CO-MEDIATORS AND TWO DISPUTANTS

It is common practice for mediators to work in co-mediator teams. This simple addition of a fourth person in mediations with two disputants complicates the number of possible emotional triangles within the mediation itself. With one mediator and two disputants, one emotional triangle exists between the disputants and only one three-person triangulation within the mediation is usually possible. With the addition of a co-mediator, the number of potential three-person triangles jumps to four. (In fact, the number of emotional triangles increases exponentially with the addition of each person to the mediation process.) These include Disputant A, Disputant B, and Mediator C; Disputant A, Disputant B, and Mediator D; Disputant A, Mediator C, and Mediator D; and Disputant B, Mediator C, and Mediator D.

In each instance, any person can occupy inside or outside positions of the triangle. The emotional reactivity of triangulation can be activated due to a number of contextual variables including race, gender, religion, socioeconomic status, etc. The following scenarios illuminate the potential for triangulation.

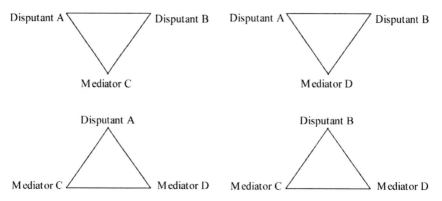

Figure 6.5.   Four Potential Triangles with Four People.

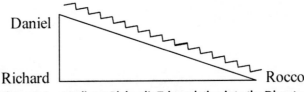

Figure 6.6.   Mediator Richard's Triangulation into the Dispute.

Two disputants, Daniel and Rocco entered mediation because of a neighborhood dispute involving a barking dog. The mediators were Richard and Cindy. Each disputant felt more comfortable with the male mediator, Richard, and so vied for the inside position with him. This took the form of speaking directly to and in other ways soliciting support directly from Richard. As the emotional intensity of the mediation increased, Richard's level of objectivity diminished, and he began responding more favorably to Daniel. Richard had been triangled into the mediation conflict, and his ability to broker a fair resolution was compromised.

Next, Cindy began to feel anxious in response to the developing imbalance between Richard and Daniel and, rather than self-soothing to manage her own reactivity, she tried to re-balance the mediation through siding more with Rocco. Rocco then began to respond positively to Cindy's overture, since, in his mind, Daniel and Richard seemed too close, and Cindy was his ticket to getting what he wanted from the mediation. A second, interlocking triangle was formed with Cindy and Rocco on the inside position and Daniel, the second disputant, on the outside position.

Things became more complicated when mediator Richard, uncomfortably sensing this allegiance between Rocco and mediator Cindy, tried to break up that coalition by undercutting Cindy's efforts. Now a third, active, and interlocking triangle had developed with Cindy and Rocco on the inside position and Richard on the outside position.

The same dynamic was replicated when Daniel and Richard occupied the inside position of a triangle with Cindy on the outside of the triangle.

While effective and experienced mediators will rarely get themselves involved in such a convoluted situation, emotional triangles and triangulation are as pervasive as they are natural, automatic reactions to escalating chronic

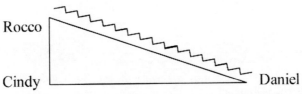

Figure 6.7.   Mediator Cindy's Triangulation into the Dispute.

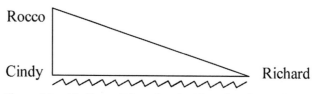

Figure 6.8.   Mediators Triangulated with Each Other and One Disputant.

anxiety. That is, everyone both creates and perpetuates emotional triangles in life. As such, we are all vulnerable to these dynamics. Furthermore, the lower the level of differentiation of the disputants and/or the mediators, the more likely triangulation will occur. As is the case with all of Bowen theory, the solution to being triangulated and the capacity for de-triangulation resides in the capability of a person to systemically see what is going on, refuse to participate, and, if caught by the anxiety of the moment, extricate himself from the triangulation. In mediation, this capacity for systems action is, of course, directly related to the differentiation level of the mediator. The higher the emotional maturity of the mediator, the less likely he will get caught initially and the more able he is to get unstuck.

As stated in Chapter 5, "Emotional Maturity and the Mediator," the first and foremost goal of a successful co-mediation team is to work together cooperatively. This entails supporting one another, following the mediation process, honestly addressing issues between themselves as they arise, and each taking personal responsibility for her or his actions. By operating on the same page, the mediators, in essence, assume the same point on the mediation triangle, such that they function as one. Even though the mediation triangle is technically considered "complicated," since the mediators occupy the same point on one side of the triangle, they function as one. For all practical purposes, the triangle is simple. By occupying the same point in the mediation triangle, however, the co-mediators create a powerful resonance that positively influences the mediation environment. Structurally, two mediators acting as one simplifies the mediation and replicates the one mediator with two disputants model described above.

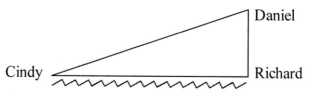

Figure 6.9.   Mediators Triangulated with Each Other and Second Disputant.

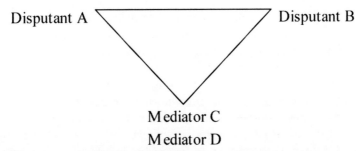

Figure 6.10.   Mediation Triangle with Two Mediators.

A solid co-mediation relationship is much less likely to fracture when tensions rise and emotional reactivity between the parties escalates. A reliable co-mediation relationship is resilient and adaptable. As trust develops between the mediators, each is able to more effectively move in and out of the mediation process. Each can take turns entering the system and retreating from the dispute as the other mediator gains a fresh perspective or is there to "rescue" the first from over-involvement or under-involvement.

While the triangle is complicated with the two co-mediators on one triangular point, the cooperation between the co-mediators shifts the focus of the mediation from the original, central triangle of the two disputants and the conflict itself to the mediation triangle. Together, both mediators work to develop rapport, and neither allows the self or other to get overly attached to positions, disputants, circumstances, or outcomes. When disagreements occur between the co-mediators, they can be amicably discussed in front of the disputants, thus modeling effective communication and problem-solving ability. If need be, the mediators can also call for a private consultation to discuss what is occurring between them.

In sum, it is the responsibility of the co-mediators to see systems and act based on what they see. Strategies for coping with a more poorly differentiated co-mediator were discussed in Chapter 5. What is worth repeating, however, is that those not capable of effective self-regulation and self-responsibility should be actively discouraged from working as mediators until and unless they make a commitment to recognize their limitations and change their behavior. Ineffective mediators stain the profession and make it more difficult to promote effective mediation and assist others.

CO-MEDIATORS, TWO DISPUTANTS, AND ATTORNEYS

With additional parties in mediation, there are more emotional triangles and an increased potential for multiple triangulations. Attorneys are often a part of mediations. They participate in a variety of mediations, including civil mediations, employer-employee contract mediations, domestic mediations, environmental mediations, and public policy mediations. Different mediators and diverse mediation programs treat attorneys in a variety of ways. For some mediators and programs, attorneys are routinely barred from participating in mediations. These mediators and programs believe that it is best for the parties to meet without attorneys. The thinking is that: (1) attorneys are trained in litigation and are usually not familiar with mediation; (2) they are taught to advocate for their clients and not to find common ground and cooperatively problem-solve, and (3), in general, the presence of attorneys impedes the parties' abilities to find their own solutions to their conflicts.

Other mediators and programs function differently. Some always include attorneys, believing that their presence can help "professionalize" the mediation by bringing in a levelheaded presence, acting as the stabilizing point for disputants too caught up in the conflict to see things clearly. Other mediators and programs take a more flexible approach, at times willing to include attorneys in mediations, but with clear guidelines about their roles and how and when they can participate. I will discuss these stances and how attorneys, even those more capable of maintaining greater objectivity, complicate triangulation processes in mediation.

In terms of adaptability and functionality, Bowen theory eschews polarization and rigid adherence to extreme positions. In fact, Friedman (1985) argues that those who hold the most extreme positions on both sides of any issue or belief have the lowest levels of differentiation. As dogma increases, differentiation level decreases, and the degree of inflexible beliefs, reactive feeling, and "mindless" actions increases. The more rigid the person, the less capacity he has for flexibility, adaptability, and resiliency.

Applied to mediation, an uncompromising stance to always exclude attorneys from mediation or always include attorneys in mediation may indicate extreme reactivity on the part of the mediator or program. Any rigid position defining *all* situations in the same way excludes the possibility of adapting to particular circumstances or contexts. A more differentiated mediator, for example, is more interested in defining the mediation process, clarifying the role and responsibilities of the participants, and reinforcing the centrality of the mediator to the mediation process than promoting all-or-nothing solutions to the problem of attorneys in mediation. In other words, a more differentiated mediator works with attorneys to define how they may be effective in mediation, rather than always including them or always excluding them. From this perspective, sometimes an attorney may be excluded from mediation if the mediator does not believe the attorney can abide by the guidelines set forth by the mediator, and sometimes the attorney may exclude herself if she believes that she is not needed or if she does not want to accept the limitations of her role in the mediation. And, at other times, the attorney may be excluded from the mediation even if she was initially included but is no longer helpful or needed.

Some mediators choose to exclude attorneys because it is easier to conduct mediations with fewer participants in the room. This is understandable, but not necessarily helpful. Some disputants will not participant without their attorneys present. In other situations, as noted above, the presence of attorneys in highly charged environments can help calm agitated clients.

Rather than simply excluding or including attorneys automatically, a mediator trained in Bowen theory recognizes the potential and pitfalls of including attorneys and actively works to minimize triangulation and promote clearheaded thinking, feeling, and acting. I will describe several scenarios that include attorneys and how they complicate the possibilities for triangles and triangulation.

One Attorney and Two Disputants

There are instances where one party brings an attorney and one party does not. This was fully described in Chapter 3, where I remarked that the unrepresented party often feels a power imbalance in the mediation. I also discussed strategies for re-balancing power and calming the unrepresented party, such that mediation can proceed in a just and balanced way. Here, I want to address how the presence of one attorney can reinforce a complicated triangle, a situation to which the mediator must be consciously aware.

In essence, the attorney enters the mediation on the side of his client and also, automatically, on the client's point of the triangle. Thus, there is an increased potential for triangulation between the attorney and her client on one point of the triangle, with the other two points occupied by the mediator and second disputant respectively.

In these instances, it is important that the mediator not battle with the attorney. That is, the mediator is advised to remain clear about the attorney's role in the mediation, the mediator's responsibilities, and the disputants' duties. The mediator must carefully avoid the automatic pull to balance the mediation by supporting the unrepresented party. By doing so, she risks triangulation with the unrepresented party and the mediator on the inside position and the attorney and represented party occupying the same point on the outside position of the triangle. If she succeeds in developing a mediation triangle with all participants, she avoids this pitfall.

Should she fail, the mediator's neutrality, balance, and objectivity is compromised and the mediation is likely to falter. Rather, the mediator's

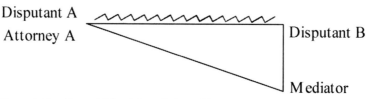

Figure 6.11.   Potential for Triangulation with One Attorney, Two Disputants, and Mediator.

challenge is to promote a mediation triangle that is complicated, meaning a mediation triangle with the represented party and the attorney on one point of the equilateral triangle and the unrepresented party on the second point of the equilateral triangle. The mediator, having made clear that the attorney's role is secondary to the active and primary role of the disputants, is thus responsible for containing a potentially rambunctious attorney, providing breaks to allow the attorney to consult with her client, and actively encouraging disputants to take personal responsibility for their situation and the mediation. As long as the mediator is aware of her responsibilities, can remain relatively non-anxious and emotionally detached, and stay actively involved, managing a mediation with one attorney can be relatively easy.

This is the same challenge with co-mediators and a single attorney. If the co-mediations are working cooperatively, and if they have mediation experience with a represented and un-represented party, the team can operate as one, occupying the same point on the mediation triangle. If, on the other hand, one or both co-mediators are unable to manage conflict, cannot reinforce roles and boundaries, or otherwise fail to perform the required duties, the mediation will likely spin out of control, with triangulation running rampant between attorneys, disputants, and possibly even the co-mediators. By following the guidelines discussed earlier with the co-mediation team and triangles, however, the participation of a single attorney need not be an impediment to a successful mediation and, in many instances, the presence of a levelheaded attorney can improve the chances for a successful mediation.

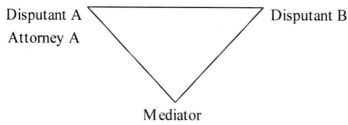

Figure 6.12.   Mediation Triangle with Two Disputants and One Attorney.

Two Attorneys and Two Disputants

While the addition of a second attorney can be helpful, especially if both attorneys are relatively professional, two attorneys in mediation can also complicate the mediation through increasing the size and scope of potential triangles and triangulation.

For example, I recently mediated a civil mediation with two attorneys, Suzanna and Alicia, who did not get along. There was significant history between the two that had erupted into a heated exchange during a previous meeting with the two attorneys and two disputants. I was not present at the first mediation, but was brought in as a consultant since the first session went so poorly. The mediator who conducted the first session had briefed me prior to the mediation. Unfortunately, due to an unforeseen scheduling conflict, I wound up conducting the second mediation session alone. While I initially felt some trepidation about the latent conflict between Suzanna and Alicia, I followed the guidelines listed in Chapter 3, clearly articulating the roles and expectations of the mediation with each attorney and disputant team separately and prior to beginning the formal mediation. While Suzanna noticeably bristled about the possibility of being dismissed should I believe that was necessary, both attorneys and their clients seemed relieved that I was firmly in control of the mediation process, that I had strongly and clearly established working parameters for the mediation, and that I was clear in my expectations regarding proper behavior and the consequences for failing to adhere to my guidelines. Ultimately, the mediation was successful, and the disputants were able to forge a common agreement. In this mediation, the attorneys' roles were minimal, though helpful, and the conflict between the attorneys was contained. In fact, after awhile, Suzanna excused herself when it became clear to her that her client was managing the conflict within a safe environment.

Two attorneys, two disputants, and two co-mediators increase the number of possible triangles exponentially. This requires that the mediators act with greater awareness of any developing triangles. While an exhaustive description of each and every possible triangle seems excessive, there are a few facts worth noting. Usually, each attorney sides with his or her client. This reduces the number of potential triangles, as each client and attorney occupy one point on a triangle. (While this is the norm, I have worked in mediations where the attorney was in conflict with his client, thus complicating matters immensely.) The primary concern for the mediators is to prevent attorneys from fighting a proxy war for their clients by over-functioning in the mediation. This is especially important with hesitant or shy disputants who might naturally under-function. In these instances, the attorney speaks for his client, attacking the other party or the other party's position, redirecting and rerouting the conflict through him.

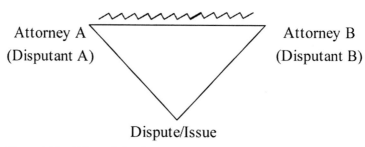

Attorney A   Attorney B
(Disputant A)   (Disputant B)

Dispute/Issue

Figure 6.13. Triangulation between Attorneys.

Should this occur, the mediation turns into litigation, fraught with legal maneuvering, and it is likely to collapse. Similarly, if one attorney begins to over-function for his client, it is increasingly likely that the second attorney will do the same for her client. Now, an interlocking triangle has developed and the disputants are both likely to under-function. As attorneys over-function, their clients tend to under-function and are thus disempowered from finding their own solutions to the conflict.

In this instance, again, the attorneys successfully reshape the mediation into a legal fight between competing attorneys, often destroying the prospects for an agreement between the parties. The attorneys "win" in that they have managed to redirect the conflict to an arena in which they may feel more comfortable and have been trained. They are also poised to reap the financial benefits that a failed mediation offers. The disputants "lose" in that they have lost their personal authority to manage their conflicts and come up with reasonable and workable solutions, and they are left as observers in a legal system, rather than as active participants who can resolve their own dilemmas. They are also, unfortunately, left with the financial tab of paying more money to their attorneys.

Here, as in most every other instance, there is no real substitute for a highly differentiated mediator. A more emotionally mature mediator is not easily intimidated by the power antics of an attorney seeking to control the mediation. Less experienced mediators may be challenged to assert their authority in controlling the mediation process, even if they are relatively well differentiated. This is why it is important that less experienced mediators be paired with experienced, well-differentiated mediators. Should less experienced mediators be paired with experienced but more poorly differentiated mediators, they are likely to feel confusion, as their natural instincts to more effectively manage the developing situation may be at odds with what they see occurring with the more senior but less emotionally mature partner.

In sum, attorneys offer the potential to bring a more objective, clearheaded perspective to the mediation. As professionals, they can be voices of reason for emotionally charged clients. They can offer reality tests for proposals and support wise options for disputants stuck in hardened positions or blind to possibilities due to their emotional attachments to the conflict. Including attorneys in mediations can minimize triangulation, decrease emotional reactivity, and provide a calm, cool assessment of the situation and proposed solutions.

At other times, attorneys may not provide reasonable advice or counsel. Some may not be familiar with mediation and so bring their rhetorical and litigation skills to the mediation, speaking for their clients, over-functioning beyond their proper boundaries, and in other ways making matters worse. In these situations, it is incumbent on the mediator or mediation team to consciously track developing triangles and actively and forcefully intervene to block attorneys' attempts to shift the mediation away from the disputants and onto them. Knowing how emotional triangles function, what drives triangulation, and how to de-triangulate when caught by the anxiety of the system provides the more differentiated mediator with the resources to control the mediation process and afford opportunities for disputants to manage their own conflicts and come up with workable, just, and balanced solutions to their differences.

STAKEHOLDER REPRESENTATIVES AND TRIANGULATION

There are times when stakeholder groups are an important part of the mediation process. This is especially true when working with organizations and groups where representatives are sent to mediation on behalf of the entire assembly. In fact, when dealing with business-labor mediations, environmental mediations, public policy mediations, and governmental-citizenry mediations of most every kind, it is too unwieldy for all stakeholders to have a seat at the table. Rather, it is more common for stakeholder representatives to attend the mediation on behalf of their constituencies. As the number of stakeholders increases, so, too, does the number of triangles and the potential for triangulation.

Experienced mediators know to expect the unexpected in mediation. Who among us has not been surprised or even shocked by the sometimes-unexpected turnaround by one party or the other in mediation? Often, just at the height of an impasse, when it looks as if the mediation will break down completely, one disputant will offer an unexpected solution or accept a previously rejected option. While these instances are not rare, they can seem unpredictable. In truth, while apparently unpredictable, these turnarounds are not really random or unexpected. If the mediator has been effective in promoting a fair and objective mediation, disputants may begin to experience some understanding of, if not actual compassion for, the other party and her circumstance. A resonance of good will often develops in mediation and, at its best, mediation can be a transformative process. With stakeholder groups, however, the problem often arises that a representative's shifting experience in mediation cannot be adequately conveyed to her stakeholder group. In fact, while the mediation participants come to experience the benefits of flexibility, develop a willingness to compromise, and acquire a capacity to move away from positions to interests and discover new options, stakeholder groups sometimes feel betrayed by their representative, often seeing their representative as having "sold out."

If this occurs, there is triangulation between the stakeholder group, the stakeholder representative, and "the other side" at different points of the triangle, with the stakeholders on the outside position and their representative and other side on the inside position.

Things can become more complex if the stakeholder group itself fractures, with some stakeholders supporting their representative and some feeling betrayed by their representative. Here, an active, interlocking triangle is formed with the pro-representative members and the representative on the inside position of the triangle and the anti-representative members on the outside position of the triangle. The greater the conflict or disagreement between the factions, the more active the triangulation and the more distance there is between the groups.

Of course, there are many variations on this (emotional triangle) theme. In working with stakeholder groups, a mediator is well advised to anticipate this challenge ahead of time and work to decrease the likelihood of triangulation between stakeholders and their representative derailing the mediation. Several strategies are effective.

First, in working with stakeholder groups, often mediators meet separately and caucus with each group and their representative prior to formally convening the mediation. Extensive pre-mediation preparation is important to allow all stakeholders an opportunity to discuss their concerns and the issues that are important to them. Also, it is incumbent on the co-mediation team

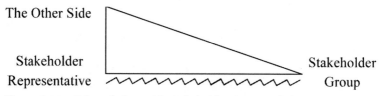

Figure 6.14.   Triangulation with Stakeholder Group, Their Representative, and "the Other Side."

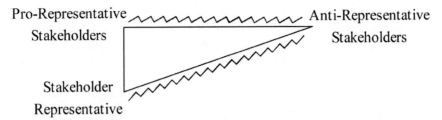

Figure 6.15.   Triangulation between Stakeholder Factions and Stakeholder Representative.

(almost all mediators working with complex mediations involving stakeholders work in teams of two or more) to carefully explain the mediation process, the dangers of working with a stakeholder representative, and the importance of clear, open communication between the stakeholders, their representative, and the mediation team. These complex mediations often take weeks, months, and even years to complete. As the mediation progresses, it is important for the mediation team to meet regularly with each stakeholder group to inform them of the general progress of the mediation (confidentiality regarding the negotiation's details may be an important issue to navigate as well), solicit their input, and encourage their support for their representative. Presenting "solid selves" to these stakeholders, that is, being well defined, self-regulated, and able and willing to develop a working relationship with stakeholders, the mediation team helps "anchor" the stakeholders, thus decreasing the anxiety in the entire system.

Also, in each stakeholder group, there will be individuals at different levels of differentiation, with some functioning with greater anxiety and thus higher levels of emotional reactivity and some operating with less anxiety and thus with more levelheaded thinking. Mediators should encourage the selection of the stakeholder representative that appears most reasonable, flexible, resilient, clear, and calm. In other words, the best stakeholder representative is the most highly differentiated member of the group. This representative may or may not be the official leader of the stakeholder group. Nonetheless, the most highly differentiated member of the group, like cream in non-homogenized milk, will often "rise to the top" of the organization. This individual remains calm in turbulent seas, is flexible and adaptive without compromising personal integrity or the integrity of the group, and has developed the capacity to relate to others and therefore can reach out across the table in an effort to find common ground, refine shared interests, and develop workable solutions to complex problems. Obviously, the more differentiated the stakeholder representative, the more likely mediation will succeed. Unfortunately, however, success in the formal mediation may not always translate to success with the stakeholders. In fact, as previously stated, a successful representative can be challenged by their groups and accused of selling out to the other side. This is particularly problematic with highly charged, emotionally polarized situations, which, in fact, represent most complex, multi-party, multi-stakeholder negotiations.

Sometimes, depending on the mediation and the number of stakeholder groups, there may be more than one stakeholder representative per group. This obviously complicates both the mediation and the relationships between the stakeholder group and the representatives. Nonetheless, the same issues remain active. Training representatives in de-triangulation techniques can be particularly helpful with these complex mediations. For example, encouraging representatives to remain calm when attacked, to find humor in situations to avoid emotional regressions, to stay focused on the self through the use of "I language" and self-responsibility statements, and to reach out to those who disagree with him rather than blaming, withdrawing, or freezing in the face of criticism all allow representatives to hold their ground and promote workable solutions in the best interests of the stakeholders and the dispute.

This training of stakeholder representatives is, in fact, an extension of what mediators ask of parties in the mediation itself. In the formal mediation, disputants are encouraged to act sensibly, use responsible language, avoid blaming, and remain open to options and new possibilities. Informing representatives and stakeholders of the pitfalls of being the representatives for the group and training representatives to more effectively communicate their thinking and actions and remaining "solid" with their convictions help these individuals assume important leadership functions for their group.

Also, there is a tendency of any group to unduly focus on the least emotionally mature member of the system. Friedman (1996) calls this the power of the dependent and eloquently describes the automatic human tendency for groups and leaders to "allow the most dependent, most easily hurt members of any organization to effectively 'set the agenda'" (p. 9). He goes on to describe that leaders and systems "promote an attitude of *adaptability towards immaturity* rather than one of responsibility, effectively shifting power to the recalcitrant, the complainers, the passive-aggressive, and the most anxious members of an institution rather than the energetic, the visionary, the imaginative, and the most creatively motivated" (p. 9). In effect, group members regressively, and reflexively, usually seek what Friedman calls "peace over progress," and thus they often undercut the very agenda they seek to accomplish.

With stakeholder groups, this particular vulnerability can be devastating to mediation. If the least emotionally mature members of the stakeholder groups hold the group hostage with their rigidity, recalcitrant behaviors, and highly-charged emotional reactivity, any progress in the formal mediation can be swiftly undercut. If the stakeholder group allows these individuals to ride roughshod over them, mediation will likely fail. This is particularly true with groups operating with a consensus model of decision-making. Friedman (1985), writing on the dangers of consensus, states, "Emphasis on consensus gives strength to the extremists. They continue to push the carrot of unity further out on the togetherness stick as the price of their cooperation" (p. 227).

With stakeholder groups and representatives in particular, the advantage of differentiated leadership become evident. A more differentiated leader-representative has a well-developed sense of self and is clear about her goals in life and for the mediation. She is less likely to falter in a highly anxious environment, is able to be both emotionally separate and linked to the group, can effectively self-regulate her own thinking, feelings, and acting, can take a stand without concern about displeasing others, and, perhaps most importantly, has developed a clear, articulate vision about where to take the stakeholder group and the mediation.

Finally, stakeholder groups operate differently regarding the authority they grant their representatives in making decisions on behalf of the group. Often, representatives must present proposals to their stakeholders for approval before any final agreements are signed. In labor-management mediations, for example, most unions must ratify any agreement before it becomes final. This division of authority has the potential to increase triangulation, as representatives seek to align themselves with their stakeholders on the inside position in an effort to either seek approval of the agreement or deflect and reject the agreement without taking personal responsibility for the negotiated settlement. If the mediation team remains connected with the stakeholder groups, they can help de-triangulate the conflict and promote solutions reached through often-difficult but productive negotiations.

Stakeholder groups and their representatives in complex, multi-party mediations can present some of the most challenging and rewarding opportunities for mediators. Multi-party mediations require advanced training, a clear strategy for implementing the mediation process with multiple representatives and groups, and, most importantly, mediators who thrive in sometimes-chaotic, emotionally intense, and ambiguous mediations. Understanding the nature of how conflict expresses itself in triangles and triangulation can provide the mediation team with a roadmap for tracking the mediation process.

For complex mediations, I find it helpful to diagram the triangles in order to track their activity and to see systems more clearly. A systems focus also has the added benefit of promoting clear thinking and objectivity in mediation. That is, if the mediators can track the conflict through triangles and triangulation, they can better focus on a plan of action for moving the mediation forward as the most active and problematic emotional triangles are addressed most vigorously. Also, the mediation team acts as consultants for each other, intervening when one or more mediators get triangled in the conflict. These processes additionally assist the mediation team to remain de-triangulated from the conflict.

In summary, emotional triangles are persistent and normal. Everyone manages anxiety through triangulation and, as such, it is a natural process of human systems. Understanding the role and function of emotional triangles and the progression of triangulation help mediators to see systems and act to de-triangulate themselves and others from emotionally-intense situations. De-triangulation promotes functional and basic differentiation for the parties in mediation and the mediator. As such, encouraging de-triangulation and the development of the mediation triangle are powerful "techniques" and strategies that help disputants find interest-based solutions to their conflict.

The following chapter discusses other strategies and methods to empower disputants and manage conflict, and it re-conceptualizes several common mediation techniques from a Bowen theory perspective.

Chapter Seven

Empowering Disputants and Managing Conflict

Ed Friedman (1996) realized the value of a well-articulated and meaningful theory in practice and in one's life. Bowen family systems theory is such a theory. Rather than an academic abstraction distinct from practical application, Bowen theory is a living theory that is equally useful, pragmatic, and relevant to one's professional life as it is to one's personal life. In fact, the central value in Bowen theory is that it does not segment the personal and the professional world at all. As such, Bowen theory integrates the personal and professional so that living the theory, that is, "thinking the theory" and applying the theory in one's professional world will improve functioning in one's personal world, *and* living the theory in one's personal world will increase one's effectiveness in the professional world. The key variable is commitment and determination. Harriet Lerner is a feminist author who has written a number of important books applying Bowen theory to a wider audience. Lerner (1989) states that learning and employing Bowen theory to increase personal and professional effectiveness is only limited by one's motivation and persistence.

In North American models of mediation, training relies strongly on techniques and methods. Although a methods-based and technique-based approach to training mediators and conducting mediations is certainly pragmatic, as an academic discipline, the field of mediation will benefit from a stronger and more comprehensive theoretical foundation. Techniques and methods devoid of theory will only advance the field of mediation to a certain point. A systemic understanding of the relative roles of the mediators and the mediating parties, as well as the mediation environment itself, will assist the profession to evolve and become even more effective, successful, and accepted. Bowen theory, as an example of extending natural systems to human systems, seems uniquely suited to provide a comprehensive theoretical model for understanding ourselves as mediators, the disputants, and the mediation process. In addition, having a stronger theoretical position will promote more success in implementing techniques and methods. The techniques and methods become ways of promoting differentiation of the disputants, de-triangling the system, increasing the functioning of the mediators, and, ultimately, creating more durable agreements. Promoting techniques and methods for their own sake seems a shallow and ineffective way of conducting mediations, as techniques and methods do not exist outside of the systemic context of the mediator and the disputants.

This chapter reviews practical applications of Bowen theory to mediation and demonstrates how employing the theory empowers disputants. Further, this chapter examines several common techniques and methods, and how the theory re-conceptualizes and applies these techniques and methods. I demonstrate how viewing and implementing techniques and methods through the lens of Bowen theory can increase the understanding and effectiveness of the techniques and methods themselves. These techniques and methods include helping disputants regain control over their conflict by learning how to more effectively self-regulate their emotional reactivity and calm their hyperarousal. Samplings of other procedures that are examined through the theory include caucusing, shuttle mediation, and brainstorming. I discuss the underlying assumptions of each technique and method from both a more traditional perspective and a Bowen theory viewpoint. I then discuss the application of these procedures through the theory.

EMPOWERING DISPUTANTS

Carron and Kenia entered mediation over an employer-employee dispute through Small Claims Court. Kenia worked for Carron cleaning commercial buildings. Kenia had injured her back, after falling on ice. Carron claimed that the quality of Kenia's work significantly deteriorated after she was injured. Carron insisted that she lost valued customers, and other clients complained about the poor quality of Kenia's work. She terminated Kenia's employment and refused to pay Kenia for her last week of work. Kenia was furious with Carron, insisting that she was exploited by Carron. She began following Carron to work, would enter the office screaming and yelling at Carron, and even followed her home on a few occasions. Carron became fearful of Kenia, believing that her "erratic behavior" was a threat. She filed a no contact order through the courts, which prevented Kenia from approaching Carron. Violation of the court order would result in Kenia's arrest. Needless to say, this action infuriated Kenia further. By the time Carron and Kenia attended mediation, emotional reactivity was running high. Carron was fearful, believing that Kenia was "unbalanced." She did not want to attend the mediation. Kenia, in turn, was outraged by both her perceived exploitation by Carron and by the no contact order. She felt that both Carron and the judge were colluding, preventing Kenia from receiving her just compensation. This mediation had all of the elements of emotional reactivity spiraling out of control.

Emotional reactivity is a pervasive phenomenon. As described earlier, reactivity is natural for all living organisms. In humans, as with many other animals, emotional reactivity is a complex phenomenon, involving biochemical and electrical processes, limbic system activations, and behavioral sequencing.

When conflict is high, emotional reactivity also escalates. At higher levels of conflict and reactivity, people often enter a "reptilian regression." That is, the more highly aroused and anxious that disputants become, the more reflexive and automatic their behavior. At a neurological level, they get stuck in and operate from the oldest, most primitive and habituated parts of the brain. Brain researcher Paul MacLean (1990) calls this the reptilian brain, the part of our brain that includes the r-complex and other "ancient" structures. Reptiles, as is well known, rely more on their instincts and accumulated, multigenerational knowledge. They are minimally capable of new learning (you don't see reptiles in animal shows for this reason), and reptiles don't laugh. According to MacLean and others, laughter and other feelings are more a function of the old mammalian brain, located in portions of the limbic system. In fact, when the amygdala is aroused or hyperaroused, emotional logic and reactivity increase. Humor is one of the most effective ways of de-escalating hyper-arousal and therefore encouraging connection, greater calm, and more lucid thinking and acting. Strengthening relationship connections between the disputants through the mediator is an important goal of mediation, especially when the parties will maintain an association after the mediation.

When a threat is perceived, stress hormones are released. In a fraction of a second, the visual cortex registers a potential threat. A direct connection to the limbic brain activates the amygdala's fight-flight response, bypassing the thinking cortex and more rational components of the brain. When this occurs, it is exceedingly difficult to think rationally; rather, more automatic, primitive reactions drive actions, as the connections between the amygdala and the motor cortex are significant. At a feeling level, the person may experience anger, fear, anxiety, rage, or other threat-related feelings. Thinking may likewise be affected, as an individual reacts with emotional logic and distorted perceptions. The outcome behavior may be verbal or physical fighting or withdrawing by freezing up or attempting to escape the situation.

I want to stress that these are all normal reactions. They have been built into our DNA over millions, if not billions, of years of evolution. These emotional and physical processes have allowed humans to survive in difficult situations for millennia. While these reactions have provided an important survival function in the past and continue to protect us in the present, there are other times when these emotional reactions interfere with more independent, thoughtful functioning. Especially in environments where imminent danger is no longer an ongoing concern, these embedded reactions can actually interfere with one's capacity for adaptability and resiliency in situations that require something more evolved than simply striking out or running away.

Mediation is one such environment. When disputants arrive at mediation, their level of conflict is usually pronounced. Differences manifest themselves in posturing and blaming behaviors as well as in feelings of anger, fear, and anxiety. Disputants are often captured by their emotional reactivity, and their thinking brains are usually highjacked by their emotional systems. Of course, the intensity and degree of their emotional reactivity are a function of their basic differentiation level and the degree of chronic anxiety present. That is, their ability to cope with the conflict is a function of their emotional maturity and personal integrity, the amount of overall stress in their lives, and their historical capacity to adjust to the acute anxiety of the presented conflict. If a person is relatively well differentiated, she has more resources, including the ability to view the conflict as an opportunity. She can better manage the stresses involved with the conflict and, with a correspondingly lower level of chronic anxiety and overall stress, she does not usually get overwhelmed with her life situation. When she does become overpowered with a particular situation, she has the resiliency to rebound more quickly and effectively.

Basic differentiation and functional differentiation levels tend to correlate. Decreased basic differentiation leaves one more susceptible to emotionally react to accumulated stress and less capable of effectively managing anxiety. Functioning is likely to spiral down, so that the present stress snowballs and accumulates. The lower the level of basic differentiation, the more inherent chronic anxiety the person carries. As such, he lacks resiliency to cope with conflict and is unable to readily recover from significant challenges. As differentiation decreases, the more likely the person will be viewed emotionally and behaviorally as a "high conflict" person. High conflict people are riddled with many physical, social, and emotional disorders. In mediation, these are the disputants (and mediators) least likely to be able to manage the ambiguity of the mediation environment. They are more prone to act out (unable to contain their outbursts, blame others, actively attempt to triangulate the mediator to his side, etc.), or act in (not show up, emotionally withdraw, or physically leave).

Most individuals do not feel particularly empowered when they feel out of control or at the mercy of another. While emotional reactive activation begins in a fraction of a second, it takes much longer to calm a person so as to re-empower him as an effective and equal partner in the mediation. To this end, the mediator must be aware of signs of amygdala activation so that once observed, the mediator does not foster further increases in reactivity. More importantly, being aware of emotional reactivity and its effects, the mediator can help disputants maintain some emotional and cognitive management of the fight-flight reflexes, thus minimizing their deleterious effects. With effective management comes the opportunity to teach and model alternative and more effective coping strategies.

Signs of emotional reactivity include physical indicators like fidgeting, interrupting, or an inability to remain silent when the other person is speaking, as well as sweating, facial expressions indicating stress and anger, looking toward the door, etc. The underlying, activating feelings involve heightened states of fear, anxiety, anger, and other "negative" states. At a behavioral level, emotional reactivity is perceived through increased levels of blaming, rationalizations and justifications, statements of being victimized, verbally attacking the other, inability to follow the directives of the mediator, and additional behaviors that reflect a lack of personal integrity. At its most extreme, emotional reactivity will lead to a full blown fight-flight reaction, including storming out of the mediation, freezing up and not being able to participate, or, in rare instances, attempting to physically assault the other disputant. Should these latter reactions occur, the mediator has lost control of the mediation process, and it is often too late to restore a working framework. Sometimes, especially when there are multiple parties or multiple stakeholders, mediation can reconvene after a cooling-off period.

To prevent this kind of potential damage, the mediator must be aware of the signs of increasing hyper-arousal and de-escalate the anxiety cascade before it has the chance to cycle out of control. For example, if the mediator sees signs of increasing emotional distress and reactivity, she can call for a break or a caucus. Sometimes, taking a quick break allows disputants to calm themselves and return with greater control over their reactions. This is especially possible with more differentiated parties. The higher the person's basic level of differentiation, the more capable she is of managing her reactions and promoting reasoned thinking over automatic emotional reactivity. As functional differentiation levels decrease, the parties might need the mediator's assistance to help calm them. Calming highly activated individuals requires more specific interventions.

Caucusing is particularly effective in these situations, especially if the mediator has been successful in promoting a strong mediation triangle such that rapport between the mediator and the disputants is strong. With a solid working relationship established, the mediator has developed credibility with the parties and can more effectively move in their worlds. In caucus, the mediator can empathize with the disputant's situation, encourage thinking over reacting, promote personal responsibility, support management of emotionality, and effectively use humor to de-escalate the conflict. By staying focused on the possibility of negotiating a workable solution and engaging the disputant both compassionately and humorously, the mediator helps quiet the activated amygdala and provides opportunities for the more thoughtful, creative parts of the neocortex to engage, thus encouraging a productive mediation outcome.

Also, in caucus, direct educative approaches may prove valuable. Discussing with the disputant exactly what is occurring physiologically and emotionally, the mediator can provide valuable information and resources to help calm the individual. Getting a person to control their breathing to shift the nervous system to a calmer state, allowing a disputant to "blow off steam" so that he can release the emotional build-up, and setting strong and appropriate limits on behavior and expression of feeling in the reconvened mediation can all provide safety. Emotional reactivity decreases as a sense of safety and trust increases.

In general, the longer the conflict, the more personal the dispute, and the lower the level of differentiation, the greater the potential for emotional activation. If, for example, a disputant can obtain some relative distance from the conflict, either because the issue is not so personal or so longstanding, or if he is relatively mature, then emotional reactivity will not likely be a significant variable in the mediation. If, on the other hand, the conflict is longstanding, for example with a protracted labor-business dispute or in a high conflict marriage where property and parental access are being mediated, then the parties are more likely to enter mediation with the conflict binding a significant amount of anxiety. In these instances, the mediator can expect high emotional activation and a possible hyper-arousal situation.

Sometimes, parties do not want to calm down. High conflict people can be very difficult to manage. They may enjoy the level of stress the conflict provides. Some take pleasure in the adrenaline rush that accompanies high conflict. Others use the conflict as a way of staying fused to the other party or the issue itself.

This was the case during a mediation with Chloe and Matt to renegotiate parenting access. From the beginning, the parents quickly escalated into blaming each other. Janet, my co-mediator, and I worked diligently to refocus the parties so that we could complete the introduction and have them tell their stories. Neither Chloe nor Matt could stay silent during the introduction and both continually interrupted each other during uninterrupted time.

They could not remain attentive to the task. Try as we might, their reactivity to each other escalated to the verge of an anxiety cascade, where anxiety threatened to rise so quickly that the parties might verbally and physically lose control. After Stage II was completed, we decided to caucus with the parents. Matt said it was hopeless. I responded that we were good at our jobs and to give mediation a chance. He responded, "You're not *that* good." We then caucused with Chloe and discovered that she, too, did not see the value in continuing with the mediation since she was so angry with Matt. Following the two caucus meetings, Janet and I discussed the case. We decided to terminate the mediation since neither Matt nor Chloe wanted to continue, and both seemed more focused on elevating the conflict than resolving it. We could not establish a solid mediation triangle, and it was clear that the parents were using the mediation to continue with a decade-long, post-divorce pattern of staying emotionally connected through tearing each other apart.

While most people would deny that their conflict might have some secondary gain or reinforcing elements, high conflict can become a kind of "superglue" between disputants, particularly those with lower differentiation levels and higher chronic anxiety. With particularly high conflict individuals like Chloe and Matt, mediation may not be appropriate and restoring safety for the parties, through physical distance, becomes the primary goal. Mediation requires the parties to have a certain ability to self-regulate, a willingness to explore the conflict and the potential solutions, and at least a marginal level of personal responsibility. Without the commitment to these basic principles and the ability to implement them throughout the mediation, mediation may do more harm than good. Those least emotionally mature and under the greatest stress may need a judge to sort out their affairs. While a judge's decision may not restore equilibrium and calm, the authority and security of the courtroom can provide greater safety than the mediation environment.

Carron and Kenia were more successful. While their conflict had all of the hallmarks of a potentially disastrous mediation, both had a genuine interest in moving beyond their conflict. Through the stages, Carron and Kenia calmed down, which allowed me to develop a mediation triangle with them. At times during the mediation, their disagreements flared and they regressed into blaming and threatening. Their willingness to take some personal responsibility for their part in the dispute, their mediation relationship with me, and their readiness to learn how to compose themselves during caucus resulted in a tenuous but satisfactory mediation agreement between them. They found common interest in wanting to move past the conflict and progress with their lives. Neither wanted to stay stuck in being angry with each other. Kenia apologized for "getting crazy" about her job loss and Carron accepted her apology. This coming together resulted in Carron's willingness to offer Kenia a modest but important severance payment, as well as an agreement to withdraw her court order against Kenia. Kenia, in turn, agreed to refrain from contacting Carron in the future. The participants learned to self-regulate their hyper-arousal under difficult circumstances and to take control of resolving their conflict. Both women developed important skills that were transferable outside of mediation, and both women felt empowered by the mediation process and outcome.

For those with a willingness to accept some personal responsibility, who do not want the conflict decided by another such as a judge or arbitrator, and who do not need the conflict as a way of defining their lives and staying connected to the other, mediation effectiveness increases. Mediation offers the opportunity to calm the system, promote rational thinking, decrease emotional reactivity, and diminish the automatic thinking, feelings, and behaviors associated with the fight-flight reaction.

As emotional reactivity decreases, parties experience a sense of their own personal authority and autonomy. Their attachment to positions decreases, they are more able to articulate their interests, they can more clearly discuss the issues in their conflict, they can engage in productive conversations with each other, and they can entertain a variety of self-generated options. When parties experience this kind of empowerment, they are less afraid, less anxious, and less fearful. Increasing empowerment decreases threat, allowing for more appropriate engagement and more personal responsibility for developing solutions. This becomes a positive feedback loop where success breeds more success. In effect, empowering disputants by helping them to minimize their reactivity, managing fight-flight reactions, and calming the system leads to more productive and successful mediations.

CAUCUSING FROM A BOWEN THEORY PERSPECTIVE

Caucusing is a technique whereby a mediator meets separately with each of the parties. Generally, the content of these separate meetings is kept confidential from the other party. From early on in the mediation literature, mediators such as Christopher Moore (1987) and Charles Bethel (1986) describe the technique of caucusing as a standard tool in the mediator's repertoire. Mediators know the benefits and dangers of using caucusing. Some use it routinely; others refuse to use it at all. Caucusing can be a powerful tool for breaking impasses. A mediator can discover important information, build stronger relationships with one or both of the parties, conduct reality testing, check for safety issues, rebalance when power is imbalanced, and in other ways determine the causes of and help to dissolve impasses. On the other hand, caucusing can also create situations in which breaking impasses becomes more difficult, especially if the mediator is perceived to be or is actually more aligned with one of the disputants. When conceptualized through a Bowen theory perspective, caucusing is a technique in which the mediator is extremely vulnerable to triangulation.

By definition, meeting in caucus creates inside and outside positions on triangles. The emotional anxiety that is a part of being on the outside position is what makes caucusing such a high-risk procedure. As a technique, mediators are trained to meet with both parties separately and for approximately the same amount of time. At a technical level, mediators know that caucusing can create the illusion of partisanship. The emotional consequence of that partisanship, real or imagined, is triangulation. Understanding triangulation, de-triangulation, and the mechanisms by which anxiety is likely to flow in mediation will assist mediators in using caucusing wisely. At its best, caucusing provides an opportunity to strengthen the sides of the mediation triangle and thus improve the relationship between the mediators and the disputants. As the parties' relationship improves, the disputants' trust in the mediator increases as well.

Not long ago, I worked with two business partners, Tyler and Logan, who were in mediation to terminate their architecture firm. During a caucus with Tyler, I found out that he was unwilling to tell Logan about his wife's insistence that she approve any agreement. Tyler reported that his wife was angry and fearful about the corporate dissolution, and she was reluctant to agree to any terms that would quicken the end of the business partnership. Tyler asked me not to reveal this information to Logan and, in fact, I had disclosed at the beginning of the mediation and again at the start of the caucus that information discussed in caucus would be kept confidential, unless the parties agreed otherwise. Tyler attempted to place me on the inside position of the triangle with him (and his wife) regarding this vital information. The degree to which I would be triangled, that is, the degree to which I would "absorb" the anxiety of the conflict between the disputants and become reactive and responsible for them, depended on my response to Tyler before the mediation resumed. In fact, the more that I would have felt trapped by knowing this information, the more the mediation would have stalled.

By refusing to get triangulated into the disputants' conflict, I left Tyler with the responsibility of managing his dispute. This is de-triangulation. Also, this strategy strengthened the mediation triangle, as I empathized with the dilemma facing Tyler. In this instance, I deemed the information as essential to the mediation process. I understood the interlocking triangle his wife's involvement created. I said to Tyler, "I respect your wish to keep this information private. However, I do not believe that you can get a mediation agreement acceptable to both parties unless this issued is discussed and resolved. How do you suggest we proceed?" This use of "I language" kept the anxiety where it belonged, with the disputant, and it freed me to respond from an unattached position, a place of more differentiated strength rather than of more undifferentiated weakness. Tyler was left with the responsibility for determining how to proceed. Eventually, the mediation resumed and Tyler disclosed that his wife must be a part of any final agreement. With this vital information on the table, Tyler and Logan agreed to proceed with settlement negotiations but wait forty-eight hours so that both could reflect on the final terms before signing the agreement. This strategy allowed Tyler (and his wife) and Logan the opportunity to review the agreement, thus keeping the mediation balanced for both disputants.

Rather than deciding when or if to use caucusing in mediation, from a Bowen theory perspective, the focus becomes *how to use caucusing as a way of promoting differentiation of the system.* If that is not possible due to the low differentiation level of the disputants, the highly reactive nature of the conflict, or both, the mediator should not use caucusing. Viewed from this perspective, caucusing is not a technique at all but an approach to implementing the goals of Bowen theory: promoting functional differentiation as a way of increasing the likelihood of mediation success.

SHUTTLE MEDIATION

Shuttle mediation consists of literally "shuttling" back and forth between the disputants in an effort to foster an agreement. In shuttle mediation, the parties are not even in the same room. The mediator meets with one party or stakeholder group, gathers important information, helps separate interests from positions, and conducts the stages of the mediation separately. Then the mediator moves to the second party or stakeholder group, replicating this process. As the mediation progresses, the mediator attempts to generate common interests, develop options, and share the disputant's needs and perspectives with the other party. If successful, the mediator can represent the interests, options, and views of each of the sides of the conflict without seeming to advocate for one side over the other. Shuttle mediation is sometimes a preferred choice for disputants in extreme conflict. It is more appropriate when disputants are not wanting to continue a post-mediation relationship and less useful when parties must continue to work together, as with business-labor disputes, environmental disagreements, and in developing parenting plans between parents for their children.

Sometimes, the differentiation level of one or both disputants is so low and/or the conflict generated by the disagreement is so intense that parties cannot occupy the same room without spiraling out of control in an anxiety cascade. As discussed earlier, in an anxiety cascade, automatic fight-flight reactions quickly accelerate, throwing one or both parties into hyper-arousal. If it remains impossible to calm the parties, or if one party (or both parties) refuses to participate in the mediation with the other party in the same room, shuttle mediation is an option.

Like caucus, some mediators never use shuttle mediation. Others rely on this too often, reflecting their uncertainty about how to manage high conflict disputants. In this latter instance, more poorly differentiated or inexperienced mediators may use shuttle mediation to manage their own anxiety and to control both the process and the disputants. Reconceptualized from a Bowen theory perspective, shuttle mediation is an opportunity to manage otherwise impossibly reactive and conflicted parties who, nonetheless, request or require mediation.

The Bowen theory practitioner uses shuttle mediation as a last resort. There are several dangers in using shuttle mediation. First, like caucus, the mediator must be careful not to get triangulated into the conflict by the disputants. In fact, this is a more significant concern in shuttle mediation than in caucus. While caucus can promote triangulation through separate meetings with the disputants, resulting in one or both parties sometimes feeling favored or disfavored by the mediator, the confidential nature of caucus itself helps minimize triangulation and promotes strengthening the mediation triangle. In shuttle mediation, by contract, the mediator is responsible for articulating each of the party's concerns and suggestions to the other. While this provides opportunities for moving the mediation from positions to interests and reframing statements to redefine the conflict and detoxify the language of each disputant, the nature of the shuttle, with the mediator presenting the suggestions, interests, and options of one disputant to the other, increases the potential for triangulation. One or both parties may feel that the mediator is siding with the other disputant as he presents the other side's stances or bottom lines, or, conversely, the mediator's empathy and support in the shuttle can be easily misconstrued as support for the disputant as opposed to support for the mediation process. In shuttle mediation, it becomes crucial for the mediator to reiterate, over and over, that she is fairly and accurately representing each disputant's wishes, rather than representing or advocating for one disputant or the other. The mediator, thus, has multiple opportunities to define his role to the disputants, a role that is consistent with that articulated at the beginning of the mediation.

Shuttle mediation also promotes a calmer working environment in an "overheated" mediation. That is, disputants in hyper-arousal rarely take personal responsibility; they blame each other for perpetuating the conflict, and they are subject to an emotional logic that fosters "mindless" thinking, feeling, and acting. Shuttle mediation provides the mediator with the opportunity to re-connect with the disputants and thus strengthen the mediation triangle. Through humor, compassion, empathy, and a clearheaded approach to managing conflict and promoting creative solutions to their differences, the mediator has the opportunity to forge agreements through the back and forth process of shuttle mediation.

Shuttle mediation works best in situations where a continued relationship between disputants is not valued or wanted. Those with ongoing contact, such as parents continuing to raise children or employee-employer disputes, are advised to find ways to talk in the same room. This may mean postponing the mediation until tempers have cooled or until the stress level of the hyper-aroused party can be lowered. For example, I worked with a parent, Maria, who was homeless, having recently left her home, husband, and children. Maria had no job and was struggling with providing her basic physiological and safety needs. Her stress level was overwhelming, and she was unable to focus in the mediation. Maria's anger and despair were catalyzing her into rapid escalations of fight-flight. In caucus, I discovered her plight and re-scheduled the mediation in two months. When Maria returned, her living circumstances had settled down. She had an apartment and a job, and she was ready and able to negotiate a parenting plan with her children's father. In this instance, rather than using shuttle mediation to forge an immediate agreement between the conflictual parents, I recognized that time and circumstance would allow for a more productive face-to-face mediation to determine the best interests of the children.

In contrast, I worked with a couple, Marlene and Stan, who were fined by their homeowners' association for failing to keep their property clean and tidy. Weeds grew prolifically on their property, dead plants were not removed, and the homeowners' association believed that the couple was acting as irresponsible neighbors. Marlene and Stan, in turn, thought that the homeowners' association was intrusive, involving themselves in areas they did not believe were appropriate or reasonable. This conflict had been escalating for almost two years. The association began by sending reminder letters, pointing out how the couple was out of compliance with the association's Conditions, Covenants, and Restrictions (CC&Rs). Marlene and Stan repeatedly ignored the homeowners' association's requests to clean up their property. Next, the homeowners' association sent letters threatening financial reprisals if the property was not immediately tended and maintained. Marlene and Stan attended the next homeowners' association meeting and lost their tempers, screaming obscenities and threats at the board members. The homeowners' board proceeded to file a fine and lien against their property, and the entire affair ended up in court. While Marlene and Stan planned on staying in their home, they did not want to speak directly to the board representatives.

For them, resolving the issue was paramount, not rebuilding community relationships. Marlene and Stan seemed either unwilling or unable to control their tempers, and during Stage II, "uninterrupted time," they could not sit quietly while Lucy and Frederick, the board representatives, related their concerns to me. As a result, I decided to conduct a shuttle mediation with the stakeholders. As the Marlene and Stan felt comfortable with me as a mediator, they could vent their powerful feelings safely, without the board representatives feeling attacked. Without the board members present, I allowed them to spew their intense anger and, afterwards, I was able to assist them in finding common interests and fashioning an agreement acceptable to both sides. For their part, Lucy and Frederick were relieved that they did not have to sit in the same room with Marlene and Stan. As volunteers serving on a board designed to improve the neighborhood, they felt resentful that their work was unappreciated and were confused as to how someone could purchase a property in a home development with CC&Rs, sign the CC&Rs agreeing to comply, and then complain when there were consequences to ignoring the tenets of the CC&Rs. Once separated, with me shuttling between them, both stakeholders groups were able to fashion an agreement. Marlene and Stan agreed to clean up their property within one month and keep their property in compliance for one year. In return, the homeowners' association agreed to remove the fine and lien after one year. The shuttle mediation successfully allowed me to de-triangulate and thus de-escalate the passion surrounding the conflict and assist the parties in addressing the issues with more clarity, focus, and calm.

In sum, when shuttle mediation is viewed as an opportunity to mediate otherwise unworkable situations, Bowen theory again provides the framework to manage the mediation in a particular way: calming a system threatened by an anxiety cascade, promoting the more differentiated functioning of the high conflict disputants, remaining de-triangulated from the central conflict, staying self-defined around one's role and responsibilities as a mediator, and fostering a mediation triangle that encourages imaginative problem solving.

BRAINSTORMING

Roger Fisher and William Ury (1991), in their classic text on principled negotiation, *Getting to Yes*, discuss the benefits and guidelines for brainstorming. They describe brainstorming as a way of separating invention from decision. The act of generating—or inventing— multiple options, including concocting wild ideas, gets disputants working "side by side facing the problem" (p. 61).

This encourages disputants to tackle the problem rather than argue with each other. Also, Fischer and Ury suggest that brainstorming, by definition a process that suspends judgment in favor of creative ideas, generates cooperation and sets the stage for expanding promising ideas into workable solutions. They argue that uncritically developing alternatives generate good will and a spirit of collaboration, which, in turn, helps spawn additional options. Further, Fisher and Ury propose that brainstorming helps shift conflict resolution away from positions and towards interests.

From a Bowen family systems theory perspective, brainstorming offers all of the advantages Fisher and Ury suggest. Through the lens of the theory, brainstorming serves other valuable functions. For example, brainstorming helps loosen the iron grip of positions, meaning the process itself helps de-triangulate people from their positions. In other words, as disputants experience the possibility of additional alternatives and explore potential solutions, their need to bind anxiety around the dispute or around a pre-established position diminishes. The mediator directs the brainstorming process, helping to lighten the mood, facilitating the outrageousness of possible solutions, and promoting a collaborative attack on the problem. In this way, brainstorming promotes development of a creative mediation triangle, as the relationship between the mediators and the parties is strengthened, and the conflict itself is de-centralized in intensity. Conceptualized and executed in this way, brainstorming ultimately fosters more differentiated functioning in the participants.

In addition, brainstorming encourages objectivity by discouraging subjective judgments about the options. This helps the disputants move away from emotional logic, which is often enmeshed in subjective stances, toward more reasoned thinking and thus intellectual logic, which advances calmness and cooperation between the parties. Greater calmness and cooperation, in turn, support a more differentiated togetherness through building good will and helping to separate the person from the problem.

Brainstorming also promotes humor and accordingly decreases emotional reactivity. It promulgates good will and collaboration. It helps disputants see the conflict through the other's eyes, deepening understanding and empathy. As compassion, consideration, and humor between the parties increase, the likelihood of a successful mediation improves as well. And, as good will develops between the disputants, the possibility of transforming the conflict and the parties also increases.

I once mediated a civil dispute between two brothers, Malcolm and Eric. Their father had recently died and left his sizable estate to their youngest brother, Carl. Carl was severely developmentally disabled, and the father believed that Carl needed the entire estate to provide for his extended and extensive care. Eric was the estate's executor, and he represented Carl and the estate in the mediation. Initially, there was a great deal of tension between the brothers. Malcolm believed that there were enough assets to ensure that Carl was well cared for during the course of his life, while leaving sufficient funds so that the other siblings could benefit from the father's estate. When we arrived at the brainstorming phase of the mediation, I posted butcher block paper and helped facilitate the brothers working side-by-side. After fifteen minutes of brainstorming ideas, the brothers began relating favorite stories of their father and the family. Malcolm calmed down enough to really hear Eric's presentation on Carl's annual medical and homecare costs projected over the course of Carl's expected lifespan. Malcolm was still grieving the loss of their father, and he had coalesced his pain into resentment against Carl. In the end, Malcolm realized that Carl needed the estate to survive, and he only asked for several items that had sentimental value for him. Brainstorming had resulted in the desired effect of having the brothers work side-by-side on the problem, which, in turn, allowed them to calm down and share both their mutual love for each other and their grief around the unexpected death of their father.

From a Bowen theory perspective, the procedure of brainstorming is seen as an opportunity to decrease automatic hostility and fight-flight behavior, increase cooperation and connection, boost humor, and help disputants address the problem rather than attack each other. Ultimately, effective brainstorming can increase the functional differentiation of the disputants through strengthening the mediation triangle, decreasing chronic and acute anxiety, stimulating humor and creativity, and providing opportunities to intellectually engage and creatively problem-solve rather than emotionally react.

In summary, these examples explain how Bowen theory re-conceptualizes mediation techniques and methods. Empowering disputants prepares those in conflict with skills at self-regulation and self-management, skills which, in turn, can be used outside of mediation. Caucusing provides the mediator with time-out opportunities to strengthen the mediation triangle and de-escalate emotional reactivity, and by so doing de-triangulate the conflict by promoting calmness and clarity. Shuttle mediation offers the prospect of mediating with those intensely hostile to each other by decreasing hyper-arousal and promoting more differentiated responding through the mediator and the mediation triangle. Brainstorming helps de-triangulate the conflict by moving from fused positions to more differentiated interests, using humor to more compassionately connect the parties, and encouraging creative, side-by-side problem solving between the parties.

From a Bowen theory perspective, many techniques and methods can be effective in promoting successful mediations. Alternatively, many of the same techniques and methods can also fail. It is not the procedures themselves that determine success or failure, it is how the Bowen theory mediator uses techniques and methods to keep from being triangled, to promote the development of the mediation triangle, to foster the functional differentiation of the disputants, to help calm the system so that the disputants can function with greater clarity, and to foster a more resonant and thus productive emotional environment between the parties.

The next chapter addresses issues of diversity in mediation and how Bowen theory addresses these human differences.

Chapter Eight

Diversity Issues and Bowen Theory in Mediation

When I served as the director of a public charter school, I encountered many people who were dedicated to doing good work in the world. From teachers, board members, parents, and community citizens, these individuals were committed to making a positive difference. At one board meeting, a parent made a speech about the importance of teaching social justice in the school. When questioned about her meaning of this term, she said that she wanted to implement a curriculum that addressed social justice and equality issues from kindergarten through eighth grade. I queried her further as to how a five-year old could understand the notion of social justice; she said that they had to learn early that there are many wrongs in the world that must be made right. As a multiple intelligences-based school, founded on Harvard psychologist Howard Gardner's theories, whose focus is on promoting and developing all of the intelligences, especially the intrapersonal and interpersonal intelligences, I remained puzzled. I asked her how her notion of social justice was different from developing and strengthening these personal intelligences, which encourage developing a healthy sense of self, teaching students' skills to work cooperatively and compassionately with all people, and providing tools to resolve conflict peaceably and cooperatively. She did not address my question but continued espousing her "mission" that social justice was the most important issue we could address with students. After the meeting, I reflected on her passion and on her attachment to her signature concern. I realized that, from a Bowen theory perspective, there are many people whose very identities are connected to their perceived notions of right and wrong, and their identification with an issue, characteristic, belief, gender, religion, culture, race, or ethnicity colors the lens through which they view the world. These characteristics or beliefs become hot-button issues that can, in fact, create barriers to accomplishing the very goals these well-meaning people have for themselves and the world.

At the risk of polarizing the current debate regarding the importance of diversity, a polarization eschewed by Bowen theory itself, there are those whose fundamental beliefs are tied to notions of difference and there are those who search more for the universalities of the human species. The current politically and socially progressive climate makes much of the differences between humans. Some, in fact, define these differences as crucial to their identity and that of others. It is easy to simplify and categorize humans into their various distinctions. Others ignore these differences entirely, choosing to see humans as all a part of the human family. These individuals would rather focus on our commonalities as a way of creating a national or even global community. While these different perspectives may provide some comfort and calm for those in search of certainty, identity, or life purpose, Bowen theory's approach to understanding culture, race, gender, class, ethnicity, religion, and other distinctions comes in at a tangent from those seeking an either/or approach to understanding these important dichotomies (e.g. male/female, this race/that race, wealthy/impoverished, etc.). Bowen theory, in fact, says that while all of these social and biological factors relating to diversity are important, they are not the essential variables in understanding individuals and their relationships. Friedman (2007) suggests that if Bowen theory is a theory with universal application as it claims, then the crucial variable to understanding functioning remains differentiation. And, as stated previously, differentiation is essentially the movement, integration, or isolation of the two life forces—individuality and togetherness—in action.

Let us explore this idea at a deeper level. Many people derive their basic notion of identity from one or more of these distinctions of diversity. A person may, for example, define herself and see her world through the lens of gender. Another person, an African-American man, for example, may define himself and his people through the perception of race. His way of being in the world and his mission in life are reflected through his racial perspective. A third person may be a devout Buddhist and come to define herself, her world, and her politics through this identification. Other women, African-Americans, and Buddhists may reject this notion of exclusivity and distinction entirely, refusing to accept that their race, gender, or religion should define who they are.

From a Bowen theory perspective, all of these factors—culture, race, gender, class, ethnicity, and religion—present opportunities for differentiation. That is, all of these variables are "togetherness" variables. Togetherness is the life force that propels us to be a part of a group. Michael Kerr and Murray Bowen (1988) define togetherness as "a biologically rooted life force (more basic than being just the function of the brain) that propels an organism to follow the directives of others, to be a dependent, connected, and indistinct entity" (p. 65). In other words, each person is biologically "driven" to be a part of a group. Membership in groups may be a part of biology, such as gender, or socially constructed, as with religion or class, or a function of multiple variables, including biology and social construction, such as race, ethnicity, and culture. It is not the variables themselves that define the capacity for differentiation, but rather *one's relationship to those variables.* Here, the individuality life force is an essential counterbalance to the innate need to connect and belong.

The individuality life force propels us towards distinction, uniqueness, and separateness. Kerr and Bowen (1988) define individuality as "a biologically rooted life force (more basic than being just a function of the brain) that propels an organism to follow its own directives, to be an independent and distinct entity" (p. 64). Thus, it is not whether one belongs to a group that affects emotional maturity or differentiation, but rather how one understands, manages, integrates, isolates, acts, or in other ways defines oneself by these variables. For example, as an Italian-American, husband, father, son, Caucasian, and middle-class man, there are many "groups" to which I belong. If my identity is defined too strongly by any or all of these distinctions, I risk being tied to a group that can restrict my emergence as an individual who is a part of and also separate from these identities. The very act of attachment to identification can undercut my efforts to attain greater emotional maturity and thus effectiveness in the world.

The process of emerging differentiation requires not so much a balance between the life forces of individuality and togetherness, but rather a dynamic equilibrium that allows simultaneously more individuality as emotional maturity increases and also a greater capacity to be a part of a group without losing "self-integrity" in the group. As differentiation increases, so does individuality and the capacity to be intimately connected with others in ways that strengthen the self *and* others. The more self-integrity we possess, the stronger our emotional presence. As personal integrity increases, so does our ability to influence others simply by and through our presence. As differentiation increases, participation in our identified group takes on the characteristic of mutual enhancement. Group togetherness is neither exclusive to one or two of these diversity variables, nor is it reactive in ways that create conflict or polarization between in-group members and out-group members. At higher ends of differentiation, one can simultaneously be a part of a relationship or group; be a separate, distinct, and unique human being; and see, feel, think, and act in ways that honor our common humanity and heritage as biological beings.

Conversely, the lesser the differentiation level, the more attachment we have to our culture, race, gender, class, ethnicity, religion, etc. and the more identification we feel to particular in-groups. Thinking, feeling, and acting on the basis of this identification "stains" the person's world like a dye, coloring it in ways that can easily distort reality. The more a person is attached to one or more of these distinctions, the more polarized her perceptions of the world as being divided into "us and them" and the greater her reactivity in defense of her beliefs and attachments.

At the extremes, fundamentalisms on the political, religious, and social right and left breed greater intolerance and fanaticism as out-groups are viewed with suspicion, caution, and even outright hostility. We see examples of this in conflicts around the world that can be traced to ethnic, religious, tribal, and nationalistic radicalism. At the worst, these cycles of violence and exclusivity can wrench entire cultures and peoples into decades or even centuries of cultural regressions as we can observe, for example, with the conflict between the Israeli and Palestinian people. At a more micro-level, it is common to see people so wrapped up in their "cause" as to push others away with their radicalism, and ironically diminish their ability to influence others, regardless of the underlying soundness of their ideas.

MEDIATION AND CULTURE, RACE, GENDER, CLASS, ETHNICITY, RELIGION, AND OTHER DISTINCTIONS

For mediators, understanding the role of culture, race, gender, class, ethnicity, religion, and other distinctions for the disputants can be useful, though, again, the mediator must be cautious not to shift the "figure-ground" relationship (the "figure" being a person's focus on and the "ground" being everything else in the background) so that these variables become central and the more crucial variables of differentiation, chronic anxiety, emotional reactivity, and triangulation become peripheral. A disputant's religion, for example, may play a critical role in his life, but the mediator must manage her reactivity to this attachment to better promote an effective mediation environment.

To illustrate, mediating in a conservative, small city in central Arizona, I encounter many people who consider themselves conservative Christians. One couple began their mediation directly questioning me about my religion. Sara and Juan were struggling with common issues in divorce and child custody. For Juan, divorce was not an option, and he quoted the Bible to press his case to Sara that she would forever be lost if she broke God's covenant in marriage. Sara was well versed in the New Testament, and she was able to justify her leaving using Biblical passages. When they asked me whether I was a practicing Christian, I avoided a direct answer and instead reflected their common interest that their religion would be respected and that I would not judge them. Keeping my focus on avoiding triangulation and developing a mediation triangle, I steered clear of reacting to their reactivity and joined them in refocusing on our common interest in developing a parenting plan in the best interest of the children. Interestingly, their common religious "attachment" did not result in a common conclusion about the acceptability of divorce. It did, however, provide a shared opportunity for each parent to bolster his and her sense of self through identification with something bigger than the self. Rather than question the pseudo-self nature of this self-concept in mediation, I instead chose to focus on how the parents' relationship with God made them stronger as individuals who could find ways to work together to raise their children. This reframing helped move the mediation forward and the parents were eventually successful in creating a mutually satisfactory parenting access plan.

As a second example, the courthouse where I work tries its best to team male and female mediators for all of the mediations we conduct, whether they are for domestic mediations, civil mediations, or victim offender mediations. By balancing the teams through gender, we better ensure that disputants do not feel overwhelmed with too many men or women in the mediation session. Nonetheless, there are times when male-female teams are not possible and teams of two women or two men conduct a mediation. I have noticed that co-mediators who over-focus on this issue of gender balance or imbalance some-times artificially create an unnecessary sensitivity in one or both disputants.

I did this once in a civil mediation with two male mediators, a male dispu-tant, two male attorneys, and a female disputant. To the woman disputant, I stated the obvious that she was in a room full of men, and I asked her if she felt any discomfort. She looked at me puzzled and annoyed, saying no, that she trusted her attorney and had no reason to believe that the mediators could not be fair with her. In this instance, my sensitivity to the issue of gender temporarily and awkwardly unbalanced the mediation process, since my re-activity was not her concern. The mediation was successful despite my initial fumble. While it is important for same-gender teams to be aware of this gen-der imbalance and track perceived discomfort for disputants, mediators can create discomfort or raise a minor concern to significant status should they, themselves, overreact to this imbalance.

As a third example, I mediated a domestic case with two Mexican-Ameri-can parents, Ernesto and Amparo. The parents came from a lower socioeco-nomic status and neither had finished high school. Ernesto and Amparo had been divorced for ten years, yet by every definition they were high conflict parents. They used the children against each other, and for years they fought through the court system to change their parenting access. While the trig-ger for the divorce was Ernesto's infidelity, they never achieved the kind of emotional separation that is a necessary component for successful emotional divorce. Their four children, of course, paid a heavy price for their continued emotional reactivity to one another.

Once again, Ernesto and Amparo were back in mediation, for the sixth time in ten years. After reviewing the paperwork, and hearing from the court administrator that this was one of those "revolving door cases," while I looked forward to the challenge they presented, I remained doubtful that this outcome would be any different than the previous failed mediations that were referred back to the judge for resolution.

After completing the introduction, which included a review of guidelines for conduct, I prepared for Stage II, "uninterrupted time." Ernesto stopped me before I could continue; he informed me that Amparo and he had come to their own agreement about a parenting plan. They reported what they decided: joint physical custody and joint legal custody, with the children rotating between their houses every other week. Respecting their wishes, I helped them construct a parenting access plan according to the documents required by the court and, less than an hour later, they willingly signed their agreement. I was curious about how they came to such an equitable and amiable agreement after a decade of fighting, so, after we completed the mediation and signed the documents, I asked them about this. Amparo said simply that they both became aware that the children were suffering from their constant battles. Two of their sons were fighting in school, and their youngest daughter was depressed all of the time. They decided that they had to move on with their lives, not use the children against one another, and provide two loving homes for their children. Ernesto said that he felt guilty that this had taken ten years to resolve, but I assured him that having both committed to reducing their conflict and working cooperatively with each other that they were offering a gift to their children and themselves.

This example is significant for a number of reasons. It demonstrates that a commitment to increasing one's emotional maturity is not a function of race, socioeconomic status, or education. It is, rather, about a willingness to accept personal responsibility, self-regulate emotional reactivity, and release attachments such as anger and bitterness. All people are capable of such emotional growth and, as mediators, we must create opportunities for that change to express itself. For Ernesto, Amparo, and me, differences in ethnicity, socioeconomic status, and education did not negatively affect the mediation. In fact, for these parents, little was required of me, except to help them construct a parenting access plan acceptable to the court. In this instance, what mattered most was the universal love that parents have for their children and the parents' willingness to elevate that love above all else. As the parents increased their emotional functioning, the family benefited.

In all mediations and with all parties, mediators are obliged to treat the participants as equal partners in the mediation, with all of the respect, compassion, and intentional focus that they deserve. While it is true that some disputants (and some mediators) might find more comfort in working with someone more like them than different from them, it is important to treat all people with the same value, friendliness, and professionalism regardless of these distinctions. In almost thirty years of professional practice in large cities and small communities, I have worked with most every sort of client and have found that tuning into people's common humanity can overcome prejudices that all people carry, mediators included. This does not suggest that a mediator should fail to address these variables if one or more is emotionally reactive in a session. In fact, competent mediators are alert for these sensitivities and reactivities during the course of conducting mediations. Rather, it is crucial that mediators understand and manage their own prejudices and misunderstandings so that they do not promote and encourage a focus on these differences when these distinctions are not central to the mediation at hand. Ultimately, focusing on emotionally shifting positions to interests, developing rapport and the mediation triangle, understanding how to manage intense reactivity, and assessing levels of chronic anxiety and differentiation are more universally helpful, as these are the variables that all people share and that matter the most.

At a more basic level, the brains and biology of all people respond and react in the same way, with many functions "inherited" from our animal cousins. Emotional reactivity, for example, may be triggered by different situations for different people, but all people share a limbic brain that responds similarly to perceived and actual threats. Those threats activate automatic processes to fight or flee, regardless of diversity differences. Higher cortical processes can help manage these reactions through repeated attempts to calm the protective portion of the brain and instill cognitive options for responding that rely on more reasoned approaches to situations. As stated previously, limbic processes are more automatic; cortical processes can become more autonomous. This is the same for all humans. The degree of success in managing emotional reactivity and increasing thoughtful responsivity is a function of a person's level of emotional maturity or differentiation and not a function of diversity issues. Variables and distinctions such as gender, religion, socioeconomic status, race, and ethnicity affect the success of cortical override based on the degree of attachment and fusion to one's identification with these variables and distinctions, and not the variables and distinctions themselves. The extent of attachment and fusion to these variables and distinctions is, in turn, affected by factors such as multigenerational history, personal experience, and genetics. These emotional processes are, however, the same for black, white, and brown people, for Christians, Jews, Muslims, and atheists, for rich and poor, and for men and women.

While much is made in our postmodern world about issues of culture, race, gender, class, ethnicity, religion, and other diversity differences, in an environment based on political correctness, these variables and distinctions can be sensitized to the point where they seem like the most important aspects in human interactions and in human systems. Though not insignificant, Bowen theory resists the "herding" impulse to attach over-importance to these distinctions. Ed Friedman (1991) suggests that these variables enrich human experience and color the differentiation process, making it more visible and variable. The richness and diversity of people and their experiences are what make the human race so wonderfully textured. Mediators are advised to approach these variables as opportunities for receptive learning and increased differentiation. We are personally enriched when we gain knowledge about people and differences. For example, issues such as oppression and coercion, which are a part of many people's lives and cultures, can motivate us to help improve the lot of humanity. And, compassion and understanding can assist us in working more effectively with people who are different. Nonetheless, Bowen theory warns us against getting seduced by these variables and distinctions so that the central concepts in understanding humans and their systems get minimized. For all humans, across all cultures, religions, and experiences, the core components of differentiation, triangulation, chronic anxiety, individuality and togetherness, emotional systems, and other systemic processes provide a more consistent roadmap for understanding how to effectively navigate the complex terrain of human interactions.

The next chapter investigates one of the most intricate, difficult, and rewarding types of mediations, domestic mediations.

Chapter Nine

Domestic Mediations, Emotional Maturity, and Reciprocal Relationships

In the United States, one of the most common forms of mediations involves parents creating parenting access plans for themselves and their children. Currently, most states either require or provide for these domestic mediations as a way of unclogging overcrowded courts, allowing parents to decide what is in the best interests of their children, and affording parents the opportunity for cooperative parenting and problem-solving. When parents are able to co-create a mutually agreed upon parenting access plan, they are usually more invested in following through with the arrangement as they develop some ownership through their active participation in crafting it. In turn, this often results in greater overall compliance and a reduction in post-decree conflict (Benjamin and Irving, 2007; Mathis and Yingling, 2005).

Should parents refuse to participate in domestic mediations to develop parenting access plans, or if they fail in crafting a mutually acceptable agreement between them, they are left with little recourse than to take their case to court where the presiding judge decides what is in the best interest of the children. Judges are usually reluctant to make these important decisions, as they recognize that they are making decisions based on limited and often skewed information. Parents in disputed child custody fights, either representing themselves or being represented by their attorneys, attempt to disparage each other, while bolstering their own parenting credentials. In many ways, this resembles the state of divorce proceedings in this country prior to implementing no-fault divorce laws. No-fault divorce laws were passed in an effort to decrease the acrimony in divorce. Before these laws were enacted, each spouse would attempt to prove that the other spouse was "at fault" for the failed marriage. No-fault divorce laws have significantly reduced or eliminated these brutal court fights regarding marital dissolution, replacing the concept of "fault" with "irreconcilable differences." Disputes regarding child access continue, however, with parents fighting for custody and access, accusing each other of verbal and physical abuse, neglect, threats, affairs, drug and alcohol abuse, and other sordid accounts designed to undercut the other parent and strengthen their case as primary custodial parent.

Judges should be commended for their willingness to hear all of the evidence and allegations and to render judgments based on their best reading of each case. While not all individuals are candidates for domestic mediations, as the most poorly differentiated parents sometimes do better in the structured environment provided by the court, court-centered child custody fights produce "winners and losers." From a mediator's perspective, however, there are no real "winners," as conflict often escalates, and the family usually "loses" as the opportunity to promote cooperation has been diminished by the emotional costs and financial expenses of the court process. As a result, disgruntled parents are less likely to follow through with the judge's court order; they often find ways to actively or passively resist the parenting access plan imposed on them. At their worst, these cases can linger through the court system for years, with one parent or the other re-filing motions for new parenting access plans, accusing each other of failing to follow through, or in other ways keeping the parental conflict alive to the detriment of the children.

Due to the often-inordinate emotionality involved in divorce or separation for parents who never married, domestic mediations can decrease reactivity, promote cooperation, and help disputants work together to raise their children in loving, supportive homes. Also, mediation is often indispensable for individuals in conflict who will continue a relationship with one another after the conclusion of the mediation. With parents, this is almost always the case, as they remain intimately involved in the lives of their children not only through the legally-mandated years when children are minors, but throughout their children's lives as they grow into young adulthood and middle adulthood. I often hear from parents how easy it is to get married and how difficult it is to get divorced. When divorce involves children, this extensive involvement with the courts and with mediation can help families construct a smoother transition to post-divorce life.

In this chapter, I investigate the phenomenon of divorce and post-relationship parenting by examining the family life-cycle issues that make divorce and separation so emotionally charged. I also discuss several relevant Bowen theory concepts to assist domestic mediators in understanding what makes spouses and parents so emotionally reactive to one another, including the differentiation levels of parents, how reciprocal relationships affect mediation, and what mediators can do to manage especially reactive parents.

THREE TYPES OF DOMESTIC MEDIATIONS

While civil mediations to divide assets and liabilities of divorcing couples can also be a part of the divorcing process, this chapter focuses exclusively on developing parenting access plans. There are basically three types of domestic mediations involving children and parenting access plans. The first scenario, and the most common, involves married parents going through a divorce. The second and not rare circumstance involves developing parenting access plans for couples who were never married and who, in fact, may have never been in an emotionally committed relationship. The third situation involves post-decree parents who continually cycle through the system. Year after year, they seek judicial solutions to their emotionally reactive lives and fail to accept personal responsibility for the long-term conflict that keeps them emotionally fused with each other in a perverse kind of emotional polygamy. First, I will examine the most common situation, that of divorcing couples in need of developing a parenting access plan in the best interests of their children.

Divorcing Couples

In Arizona and in many other states, parents must complete a parenting access plan before the court will grant a marital dissolution. Parents are also required to attend parenting classes, which discuss the emotional and legal aspects of divorce, what to expect as parents negotiate the legal system, how divorce affects children, and what steps parents can take to decrease the negative influence of divorce on children. These parenting classes are almost always universally praised by divorcing couples, as many parents come to realize that the quality of their relationship with each other as parents and their continuing or developing relationships with their children are the most significant variables for healthy adjustment to post-divorce family life.

While many parents understand these ideas intellectually, many also experience difficulty in applying them to their own situations. For most couples, separation and divorce is a painful and sometimes temporarily debilitating experience. The divorce may come after a brief marriage or a long marriage. Emotionally charged circumstances may include affairs, alcohol or drug abuse, physical or verbal abuse, emotional neglect, financial dislocation, and other betrayals, denials, and painful situations. Feelings run high, including those of abandonment, anger, hurt, confusion, resentment, and even hatred. In essence, the dream of a long-term, successful marriage is over, and the rending apart of the couple causes emotional bleeding. The intensity of the grieving process and the subsequent emotional reactivity that accompanies it is often a function of the couple's unrealistic expectations about what marriage is and what it can provide.

For example, family systems psychologist Augustus Napier (1979) describes how people often enter marriage unconsciously expecting their spouses to compensate for the parenting that they never fully received in their original families. As differentiation levels decrease, dependency needs increase such that, rather than marriage as a union between two relatively whole and functional individuals, each person expects the other to "complete" him or her in order to bring happiness, contentment, and fulfillment. At the lowest levels of differentiation, young people may use marriage to escape from abusive or neglectful environments in their original families. These unrealistic expectations can never be adequately met, of course, as each person seeks from the other what is most maturely acquired from developing a solid sense of one's self. Over months, years, or even decades, disappointments build, conflict either goes underground or flares up between the two, and the couple moves further apart.

Paradoxically, the emotional fusion between the couple keeps them tightly bound to each other. Physical, emotional, and sexual abuse, affairs, alcoholism and drug misuse, severe conflict, financial disagreements, and a host of other individual and relational symptoms do not alter this basic pattern. In fact, social, emotional, and physical symptoms, as examples of emotionally-driven reactivity and triangulation, merely exacerbate the fusion between the couple. These symptoms temporarily contain escalating levels of chronic and situational anxiety. Eventually, some tipping point is reached that spills out the accumulated anxiety, flooding the couple in an anxiety cascade leading to the filing of divorce papers.

A central, basic concept in Bowen theory is helpful in understanding this process and working with parents in mediation. Bowen theory suggests that people marry at the same approximate level of basic differentiation (Kerr and Bowen, 1988). That is, the level of emotional maturity and immaturity in a couple is essentially the same. Spouses have, in effect, the same level of dependency needs, capacity (or incapacity) for intimacy and closeness, and the same level of solid self and false, pretend, or "pseudo" self. Through a complicated process of reciprocal relationship dynamics, couples will "borrow and trade" self such that one may actually appear more capable and "functional" and one may appear less capable and more "dysfunctional." Think of this as an emotional teeter-totter. Couples are emotionally interlinked. As the level of emotional maturity decreases in couples, the more variance appears between each member's functioning, with one spouse often "going up" on the seesaw, looking more capable, and the other spouse "going down" on the seesaw, looking less capable. Each spouse's position is dependent on the other spouse's position on this emotional teeter-totter, so that the couple "borrows and trades" self, with one spouse going up in functioning as the other spouse goes down in functioning and visa versa. This borrowing and trading of self may sound almost mystical. It is, rather, part of what Lerner (1989) calls a "dance of intimacy," which describes how married partners navigate the turbulent and calm waters of their relationship. Family therapist Peggy Papp (1994) says that more extreme reciprocal relationship patterns can coalesce around a number of themes, including teacher-student, caretaker-patient, alcoholic-enabler, "saved"-sinner, etc., all of which are variations on the theme of over-functioning and under-functioning.

All couples experience over-functioning and under-functioning aspects in their relationships. Couples at higher levels of differentiation, however, are more fluid and flexible with these arrangements, so that rigid patterns do not develop that undermine the viability of each other or the marriage. With more emotionally healthy couples, these patterns are more transient and fluid; they enhance family functioning rather than undercut the emotional efforts of spouses or children. For example, a more emotionally mature couple might divide child care responsibilities so that the wife is primarily responsible for an infant and the husband is principally responsible for a toddler. Or, the husband is predominantly responsible for cooking, and the wife is chiefly responsible for household finances. Each utilizes his and her strengths, respects and appreciates the work of the other, experiences competence, and constructively contributes to the life of the family.

As differentiation levels decrease, patterned behaviors and roles become more pronounced and rigid. In addition, in-laws, affairs, work, children, substances, and a host of other anxiety-binding symptoms actively triangulate into the marriage, undercutting the emotional functioning and thus the independent and interdependent capacities of both the spouses. One spouse, and sometimes both, begins to feel constricted by the marriage, blaming the other for the difficulties. For example, feeling trapped, the wife may seek the support of friends, family, or a lover for validation. Distance grows as disappointments mount. These symptoms of marital troubles are actually a reflection of the fusion in the relationship. That is, rather than taking personal responsibility and adopting a self-focused attitude for having co-created the marriage and resolving the difficulties that exist, each spouse uses other focused, blaming reactions to escape the responsibility for a failing marriage. As accusations increase, opportunities to resolve conflict reciprocally decrease.

Marriage psychologist and Bowen theorist David Schnarch (1997) describes these common challenges in marriages as normal and exciting opportunities to grow both individually and relationally. He believes that marriage is uniquely suited to foster emotional development. Rather than taking this opportunity to transform themselves and their marriage into the kind of relationship that could actually provide the happiness originally conceptualized, however, many couples endeavor to escape their marriages and, thus, undercut their own ability to become more effective, happy, and emotionally mature people.

While there are certain situations that demand an immediate response of leaving, such as marriages where abuse and domestic violence is ensconced and endemic, Schnarch (1997) believes that the crucible provided by marriage provides a golden opportunity for breaking free of constricting definitions of the self and the marriage. He proposes that emotionally maturing does not necessitate breaking up. In fact, when spouses attempt to escape their marriages in an attempt to "grow," the usual effect is just the opposite: people remain entangled in emotionally reactive patterns of hurt, disappointment, and lack of trust. They often shift the focus of those emotional reactions from their roles as spouses to their roles as parents. Especially for those with moderately low or poor levels of differentiation, this emotional fusion can last for years and through second and even third marriages. In addition, this kind of emotional reactivity can reverberate through future generations, and the reactions themselves are often echoes of struggles from generations past. New romantic involvements and remarriages without adequate emotional divorce make matters worse. Oftentimes, ex-partners become emotionally polygamous, never actually releasing their emotional attachment to the former spouse, as hate and anger are simply mirror reflections of love. Those achieving a true emotional divorce experience either an indifference to their former spouses or retain a mutual caring about each other based on the best interests of the children and the fact that they once loved each other and shared good times as well as bad times.

The notion of equal levels of differentiation in marriages is particularly useful for the domestic mediator. For me, it helps to keep the focus on the mediation itself, rather than getting distracted about who is the "better" parent. If Bowen theory is correct, both parents are equally capable (or incapable) of effectively parenting based on their similar levels of emotional maturity. As the spouses begin the process of physical separation, reciprocal relationships can shift and the under-functioning spouse may begin behaving more functionally outside of the marriage.

For example, I recently mediated a domestic case with Barb and Linde. Barb was recovering from metamphetamine addiction. For years, Barb and Linde had, what systems theorists and marriage researchers William Lederer and Don Jackson (1968) describe as a stable-unsatisfactory marriage. The methamphetamine addiction created a triangulation with Barb on the inside position with the drug and with Linde on the outside position. For years, the emotional triangle was active but fairly stable. Linde over-functioned as a typical "enabler," doing too much, covering for Barb at her work and with family and friends. As is typical of an addict, Barb under-functioned. She was rarely available for her children, her husband, her work, or herself. This pattern was interrupted by Barb's recovery. As she improved and began to function at a higher level, the emotional triangle and then the marriage destabilized. Linde's established role as an over-functioner was threatened and the stable-unsatisfactory marriage shifted to what Lederer and Jackson (1968) depict as an unstable-unsatisfactory marriage. As the triangulation with meth lessened, underlying difficulties of control and power came to the surface. Linde, comfortable with controlling everything except Barb's drug use, was unable to give up his role of manipulating the family and the marriage. Barb began refusing to concede personal power and authority to him. In fact, she began demanding equality in areas of childrearing and finances. During the mediation, it was evident that while Linde initially "appeared" more differentiated—he had held the family together for years during the addiction phase of the marriage—his level of emotional maturity was equal to that of Barb's in his more limited capacity for resiliency, adaptability, and overall functioning. Without the drug involvement and through her recovery, Barb's level of functioning began rising dramatically so that by the time the mediation convened, she seemed, on the surface, the more capable parent. In essence, Barb was "taking back" the self she traded to Linde. Linde, in turn, was "losing" the self he borrowed from Barb.

Understanding Bowen theory helped me check my impulse to support one parent over the other, as I realized that the children needed a consistent relationship with both parents, and both parents were struggling with identity, personal authority, emotional fusion, and the automatic impulse to triangulate the children into their unresolved and unevolved emotional entanglement. Knowing that both parents were equally responsible for what they co-created, I avoided getting emotionally triangled into their conflict. As a result, I was better able to remain calm, stay clear regarding my expectations, keep them focused on developing greater personal responsibility through the use of "I language" instead of blame displacement, and help the parents find common ground regarding the central issues of developing a parenting access plan in the best interests of their children. My capacity for impartiality, objectivity, and passionate non-attachment was strengthened through understanding and applying Bowen theory to this challenging mediation.

As stated previously, the loss of a marriage can be devastating, regardless of a couple's overall level of basic differentiation. Part of the mourning process involves the loss of the marriage as well as the loss of what the marriage might have become. In effect, the grieving concerns the past, the present, and the possible future. Bowen theorists and family therapists Betty Carter and Monica McGoldrick (1989) discuss dislocations in the family life-cycle, of which marital dissolution is one significant example. On page 22 of their book, they present an excellent summary, in tabular form, which describes all of processes and outcomes required for emotional divorce and the transition to a post-divorce family. They describe the "emotional processes of transition" required for successful family evolution, and the developmental issues that must be confronted and overcome. I will summarize their important findings.

The first and foremost sub-phase of divorce is "the decision to divorce," and the emotional processes involved are "acceptance of inability to resolve the marital tensions sufficiently to continue the relationship." While this may sound relatively easy to many divorcing couples, or at least for the petitioner who initiated the divorce proceedings, the requisite developmental issue, "acceptance of one's own part in the failure of the marriage" often requires significant time and effort. The more common stance is to project blame onto the other for the failing marriage. In many ways, this is easier than struggling with how one personally co-created a failed marriage. Nonetheless, by accepting one's role and responsibility for the failed marriage, the spouse is better prepared to learn from the experience, not repeat the pattern in a subsequent relationship or marriage, and work more cooperatively with the other parent in the best interests of the children.

Carter and McGoldrick describe a second sub-phase, "planning the break up of the system." They indicate that couples are required to support "viable arrangements for all parts of the system" so as to "work cooperatively on problems of custody, visitation, and finances." That is, divorce requires an emotional, financial, and logistical separation. Those who successfully navigate these developmental tasks, or who are at least willing to genuinely try, are promoting an atmosphere of cooperative problem-solving. In truth, it takes years for families to transition through all of these sub-stages to develop emotionally, physically, and financially separate households; nonetheless, parents who are committed to conducting their affairs with the least amount of blame and the greatest measure of personal responsibility improve their own and their children's chances for a successful transition. Those who remain embittered, blame the other parent, and refuse to accept personal responsibility for their actions are least likely to successfully transition to a post-divorce family.

The third sub-phase listed in Carter and McGoldrick's summary table is the separation itself. They describe the key prerequisite attitude as twofold: a "willingness to continue cooperative co-parental relationship (and) work on resolution of attachment to spouse." Again, this resolution of emotional attachment is an ongoing process but if the ex-partners realize that establishing themselves as separate individuals outside of the marriage takes priority over trying to hold onto the other through anger, bargaining, or triangulating the children, then the process of emotional, financial, and physical separation occurs more smoothly. They describe the developmental tasks of this phase as "mourning the loss of the intact family...restructuring marital and parent-child relationships...(and) adaptation to living apart."

Finally, Carter and McGoldrick's fourth and final sub-phase of divorce is the divorce itself. Here, they describe the emotional process of transition and the prerequisite attitude as overcoming intense and lingering feelings around the marriage, with the developmental issues as "mourning loss of intact family: giving up fantasies of reunion (from parents as well as children)... retrieval of hopes, dreams, expectations from the marriage, (and) staying connected to extended family."

As is evident from Carter and McGoldrick's developmental schema, divorce entails managing many emotional, financial, social, and physical factors. It is an inherently stressful time for all, and the degree to which parents can remain composed and focused, self-regulate their intense feelings, seek support from family and friends, and accept personal responsibility is the degree to which they and their children can successfully move through these stages. Knowing the stages of divorce, the emotional processes of transition, and the developmental stages required for successful divorce are important for both mediators and spouses. Divorcing spouses often feel as if their world is crumbling. They are trying to manage their heightened anxiety and traverse the unfamiliar and sometimes alien environment of the court system. They often feel out of control, with judges, attorneys, and the bureaucracy of the court process itself baffling and overwhelming. Mediation can significantly contribute to empowering parents through this legal process. As mediators, we can normalize their feelings and experiences. We can acknowledge these emotional challenges and approach parents with compassion and hope, so that they can better focus on the best interests of their children. Also, domestic mediation provides parents with the opportunity to take charge of their lives, to support their children, and to make more positive decisions in shaping their post-divorce life. In effect, a successful domestic mediation creates a parenting access plan that facilitates the transition from an intact family to a post-divorce family and helps parents begin the challenging responsibility of working together to ensure that the divorce minimally impacts their children.

Parents Who Never Married

The second scenario is increasing in occurrence. This circumstance involves developing parenting access plans for couples who never married and who, in fact, may have never lived in an emotionally committed relationship with the other parent. Growing numbers of parents attending mediation in our court system have never been married. Some have lived together for various lengths of time, usually for short durations. For many, a child is a product of a brief sexual relationship or a one-night stand. For those parents who were in an emotionally committed relationship but who were never married, many of the earlier observations about divorcing couples apply. These couples, both homosexual partners who are not permitted to legally marry and heterosexual couples who chose not to marry, are generally at about the same level of emotional maturity. They have developed reciprocal relationships patterns that may mask functional capacity. They must transition from a committed relationship to a post-committed relationship in similar ways that their married counterparts are challenged. And the involvement of both parents often means that both want maximum access to the child. Conducting mediations with these parents tend to follow the same pattern as implementing mediations with married couples, and the work of the mediator is similar.

For those children who are a product of a brief sexual liaison or a one-night stand, there are different issues and concerns to examine. While these parents usually love their children, for many parents, especially young ones, the child was not intended, may have interrupted educational plans or relocation arrangements, or may be infringing on their sense of independence. Each parent's emotional maturity level will dictate how they respond and react to their parenting obligations. Some of these parents rise to the occasion, committing to their children physically, financially, and emotionally. In fact, for many of these parents, having a child often shakes them into assuming more emotionally mature behaviors, such as relinquishing binge drinking and other party behaviors in favor of assuming greater responsibility towards themselves and their child. For others, the imposition of a child in their lives creates intense anxiety, as they struggle with what it means to "grow up" and accept personal responsibility for bringing a baby into the world.

Unlike those in emotionally committed relationships or those who have married, the basic level of differentiation of parents in brief, sexual liaisons that have created a child, especially if that encounter was a one-night stand, may be very different. These differences in emotional maturity can sometimes affect how the parents present themselves in mediation and what needs to occur in the mediation. As an example, I recently co-mediated a session with Patty and Steven, who were never in an emotionally committed relationship. The child was a product of a one-night stand. Both parents were in their late teens when the baby was born. Steven had spent time in prison, and Patty had raised their daughter alone for the past three years. Patty had filed for child support, which brought the case to mediation in search of developing a parenting access plan. When Patty and Steven arrived at mediation, neither had attended parenting class, and neither had attorneys representing them. As a result, neither Steven nor Patty had the necessary information to make decisions in the best interest of their daughter. When we were discussing legal custody, for example, neither was aware that both parents already had joint legal custody. Patty was acting as if she had sole legal custody when she spoke to the father and the mediators. Also, Patty wanted to control Steven's physical access, and neither parent was aware of the current county guidelines for parenting access plans. As a result, Patty and Steven could not make informed decisions around their Best Alternative to a Negotiated Agreement and their Worst Alternative to a Negotiated Agreement. After consulting with my co-mediator, we decided to postpone the mediation until after the parents had attended the parenting class, and we recommended that both parties seek legal counsel before proceeding. With their permission, we rescheduled the mediation.

With parents who were never committed as a couple, it is sometimes very obvious who the better parent is. In these instances, it is important for the mediator to suspend judgments and remain as objective, balanced, and impartial as possible. This can be challenging, especially if one parent is unmistakably more emotionally capable and mature than the other. During these times, it is essential to remind ourselves that our job is to follow the stages, trust the process, foster a dialogue between the parents, and facilitate an agreement that the parents believe is in the best interests of the child, regardless of how we might feel about their decisions. As always, our responsibility is to assist the couple in crafting an agreement that promotes consistent and quality time with both parents.

Revolving-Door Parents

The final scenario involves parents who continually cycle through the system year after year, seeking judicial solutions to emotionally reactive situations and failing to accept personal responsibility for the long-term conflict that keeps the parents emotionally fused with each other. These post-decree mediations are often the most challenging.

In Arizona, when a parent re-files with the court seeking new parenting orders or a change in child support, they are required to attend mediation to develop a new parenting plan. Sometimes a parent wants more time with the children as a way of decreasing her own child support payments. Or, one parent may be attempting to prevent the other parent from moving out of the area with the children. Some parents may simply want more time with the children.

In most situations, though, parents who are repeatedly involved with the courts are those that Friedman (1991) describes as the least emotionally mature and thus the least capable. They triangulate their children into their chaotic and emotionally-fused system, and over time, many of their children also become symptomatic. These revolving-door parents are often involved with other social and judicial systems. They may have legal charges pending, they may be on probation, and they and their children often have a variety of psychiatric, social, and physical symptoms. These parents represent some of the lowest levels of differentiation in society. They routinely employ blame displacement and fail to accept any personal responsibility for their circumstances. They see themselves as victims of the other parent, the courts, and other agencies that seek to assist them or hold them responsible and accountable. They have triangulated courts, schools, social service systems, family, friends, symptoms, children, and other anxiety binders into their highly reactive system. Their failure to attain a measure of an emotional divorce and their inability and unwillingness to assume even a modicum of personal responsibility leave a wake of destruction. Their children are at the greatest risk, as their parents continue to "fight it out" through them. These parents are also the least fun with whom to work.

Susan and I recently co-mediated one of these cases. Rhonda and Miguel had five children, four of whom were still minors. They had been divorced for nine years, had been through the courts innumerable times, had filed orders of protection and restraining orders against each other, and were once again back in mediation. Neither parent could be in the room with the other parent without both of them verbally exploding. Miguel had recently been arrested for violating an order of protection, and Rhonda's brother had initiated a physical altercation with Miguel to warn him to stay away from his sister. Each accused the other of abusing drugs, and Child Protective Services was already investigating the family. Rhonda and Miguel insisted that the mediation be conducted as a shuttle mediation, so that they did not have to share a room with the other. Susan and I quickly realized that these parents were among the most poorly differentiated, with the lowest levels of emotional resiliency and the highest levels of reactivity. As we proceeded with the shuttle mediation, we began making progress on the issues of summer visitation and weekend access for Miguel, as these were the concerns that brought them into mediation. We narrowed the gap between their original positions through reframing, detoxifying language, focusing on interests, developing a mediation triangle, and other common techniques in our mediation repertoire. After three hours, it appeared as if an agreement was possible. We drafted the language of their agreement and presented it to Miguel. Rather than addressing the imminent agreement, Miguel decided that he wanted to re-examine the entire parenting access plan and demanded primary physical and sole legal custody, something that, up until that moment, he had not even addressed. Susan and I called for a private consultation with each other. During our conversation, we both agreed that Miguel was not truly interested in a mediated solution and had filed anew with the courts in order to stay emotionally engaged with Rhonda by triangulating the children. Understanding Bowen theory, we also realized that both Rhonda and Miguel equally contributed to this ongoing emotional fusion as each had an active restraining order against the other and both had re-filed with the court several times in the past two years, seeking judicial solutions to issues that were essentially emotional. We met separately with Rhonda and Miguel to test our hypothesis, and then we dismissed them from the mediation.

There are no easy solutions for working with these highly reactive and problematic parents. The best that the mediator can do is to decrease her own reactivity, stay attentive to the mediation process itself, release expectations for an agreement, insist that the parties remain respectful of each other and the process, and, in general, remain in firm control of the mediation. Occasionally, a partial or full agreement is possible, as was the case with Ernesto and Amparo in the previous chapter. More often, mediation becomes a "way station" to a court date with a judge, where they can continue to blame one another for their misery and for the symptoms displayed by their children.

Parents at the lowest levels of differentiation also have the least capacity to make informed decisions, accept personal responsibility, and break the bonds of fusion that initially attracted each to the other. In a second case, the emotional reactivity between Ethan and Nadia had become so severe that the children were caught up in a domestic violence incident that resulted in one child being injured. In this situation, Child Protective Services was brought in, and the children were removed from both parents and placed with a foster family. Ethan and Nadia were given intensive and extensive services in an effort to assist them in developing the necessary skills and behaviors to effectively parent their children. This included anger management classes, domestic violence education, job training, and a host of other services. When I was brought to the case as a way of transitioning the parents to domestic mediation, there were ten people in the room! This included two mediators, the parents and their attorneys, the children's attorney, the Child Protective Services representative, and other advocates for the children and the state. The cost to the state was staggering, and I was reminded of Friedman's (1996) observation of "the power of the dependent," such that the least capable receive the most attention and services. While this is not always negative, in a society with limited resources, this kind of priority tends to deprive services and opportunities to those who may actually benefit from them. Also, since these individuals are also those least capable of changing, I wondered whether this plethora of services would eventually do anything for the children, as attorneys aggressively advocated for their clients, and only the co-mediators were advocating for the family system.

Perhaps this assessment and the subsequent examples seem unduly pessimistic or negatively self-fulfilling. Of course, hope is essential, even for those who continue to sabotage their lives and the lives of their children. Nonetheless, in these situations, perhaps more than in most, the emotional maturity of the mediator is a crucial variable. If the mediator can establish clear conditions for the mediation, work to facilitate development of the mediation triangle, and release any attachment to an outcome, then his compassion, calmness, respect, and interpersonal capacity may help raise the bar for more appropriate participation and negotiation between the parents. Change *is* possible, though, paradoxically, it is best facilitated through the mediator's emotional detachment from the outcome. The danger is that the mediator will be swept up in the drama or begin to over-function or under-function out of anxiety. The opportunity for the mediator is to use these chaotic systems to learn more about himself and develop greater capacity to fully engage without assuming responsibility for the outcome or the disputants themselves.

In conclusion, domestic mediations are one of the most rewarding types of mediations. When successful, parents not only leave with a mutually agreed upon parenting access plan detailing where the children will live and how they will be raised, but the parents also leave with greater hope that increased communication, cooperative problem solving, and a successful transition to a post-divorce family living in two households are distinct possibilities. Parents are empowered as they take charge of the most important and lasting outcome of the marriage—raising healthy children to become productive and involved citizens. Understanding critical aspects of Bowen family systems theory relating to differentiation levels of couples, reciprocal positions, and emotional fusion help guide mediators in staying focused on the mediation, not getting distracted by the sideshows parents sometimes present, and not being attached to positions or outcomes. Once again, we observe the critical importance of using Bowen theory to increase mediator self-management and clearheaded thinking for the success of mediation.

So far, I have concentrated on understanding and applying Bowen theory to mediation. The next chapter changes the focus by applying Bowen theory to a different alternative dispute resolution process, that of marriage conciliation.

Chapter Ten

Bowen Theory and Marital Conciliation

In Arizona, a marital conciliation meeting is granted when either the petitioner or respondent in a marital dissolution proceeding believes that there is a basis for marital reconciliation. In an effort to support the institution of marriage, Arizona state law grants the married couple a mandatory conciliation session that involves the petitioner, respondent, and court conciliator. The goal of the conciliation meeting is to determine whether or not there is a basis for marital reconciliation.

By the time the couple has arrived at conciliation, the marriage is severely damaged. Hurt and angry feelings abound with accusations of betrayal, disappointment, and blaming as common themes.

Although I have been conducting mediations for decades, in 2001 I began conducting marital conciliations with no formal training other than my experience as a mediator, family psychologist, and marriage and family therapist. Arizona state law specifies that conciliation is not marital counseling, so there were no guidelines for how to proceed. During my first conciliations, I stumbled around, trying to find a useful model with which to conduct these interviews and interventions. As I gained more familiarity with conciliations, however, I realized that although my background as a mediator was useful in organizing the structure of the sessions, it was my experience as a family systems psychologist and marriage and family therapist that was most helpful in guiding my assessment and intervention strategies. As such, I began to conceptualize my role in conciliations as expert consultant, assessing the couple's individual and systemic functioning and providing each person separately and the couple together with my observations regarding their significant strengths and the challenges facing them individually and relationally. Over time, I developed a procedural framework, while relying on my theoretical perspective as a systems practitioner. This chapter presents my six-stage model for conducting marital conciliations based on Bowen family systems theory.

APPLYING BOWEN FAMILY SYSTEMS THEORY TO MARITAL CONCILIATION

Marital conciliation is a brief, time-limited opportunity to assess the couple's relationship system and help them decide if there is a basis for reconciliation. The role of the marital conciliator is that of systems consultant and not marital therapist.

By the time a couple enters into court-ordered conciliation, a host of systems dynamics are active. For example, under-functioning/over-functioning patterns are often polarized, calcified, and externalized such that the marital patterns are chronically locked. Often one spouse is more symptomatic and the other is more enabling. In fact, drug abuse and alcoholism are common, as are process addictions, such as gambling and affairs. The build-up of chronic anxiety in the system, the intensity of the couple's emotional reactivity, the severity of symptom development, and the resultant polarization of their positions has resulted in an anxiety cascade and a systems collapse. This is what typically occurs when a relationship breaks down and a couple is seen in conciliation.

It is common for spouses to reactively over-focus on the other partner in the relationship instead of concentrating on their own expectations, goals, dreams, and self. Other-focused thinking, feelings, and behaviors are the norm and are manifested in blame displacement, anger, fear, and other fight-flight and defensive reactions. Neither husband nor wife is accepting personal responsibility for the marital conflicts. Reactive criticism commonly takes the form of creating distance as a way of managing anxiety or of relentlessly pursuing and blaming the other as a way of getting the spouse to change. Both approaches minimize self-responsibility by emotionally reacting to the other instead of thoughtfully responding to what it is each must do to increase self-soothing, self-management, and personal responsibility.

Other-focused thoughts, feelings, and actions often result in subjective thinking, which is thinking that is driven by anxiety and fear. All too often, subjective thinking has one or both partners believing that if the marriage ends, so will their problems. A common example of subjective thinking is: "If I cannot get my partner to change, I can change partners, or at least get out of the marriage as a way of restoring my life." Unfortunately, divorce rarely ends the pattern. If there are children from the marriage, divorce often increases the emotional intensity between the couple through triangles created with the children. Without intervention, and especially with more poorly functioning parents, blame displacement, fighting a proxy war through the children (using the children as a weapon against the other), and other forms of emotional entanglement and fusion can last for generations. In these instances, children experience escalating anxiety and often develop symptoms. They feel conflicts in loyalty between themselves and their parents and/ or their parents' new partners, and they may manifest impaired intimate relationships as they get older. Heightened reactivity results in emotional polygamy for the couple, escalating chronic anxiety for the parents and the children, and a psychic battlefield littered with casualties.

Even when a marriage is childless, escape into divorce rarely results in increased emotional maturity, as patterned responses are usually not relationship specific but, rather, stylistic and automatic. As such, using conciliation to highlight these emotional processes can help the couple recognize the relationship patterns that they have created together, each person's responsibility in developing and perpetuating the charged emotional field, and each one's challenges in decreasing emotional intensity and increasing personal responsibility. The conciliator acts to shift the couple from this other-focused perspective to a self-focused perception, that is, to help them concentrate on changing self rather than changing the other.

The conciliator must also sort through the couple's central and interlocking triangles. Common central triangles include the couple and an affair, alcohol, drugs, physical, social, and psychiatric symptoms, children, and multigenerational legacies of violence and abuse. Familiar interlocking triangles include interested friends and family members all too willing to advise and support one spouse against the other, work, money, pets, the house, and other people, places, or things caught up in the couple's struggle. At the extreme, emotional triangles saturated with chronic anxiety decrease functional differentiation and increase automatic or "mindless" reactivity. The intensity of triangulation processes can lead to the ultimate system breakdown of divorce.

Of course, the same patterns used outside of the conciliation are brought into the conciliation as husband and wife automatically vie for the "inside position" of the emotional triangle with the conciliator. To be effective, the conciliator must remain de-triangled; in other words, she must not take sides or absorb the anxiety in the couple's relationship. The conciliator must establish and maintain a balanced working relationship with each spouse. Similar to the mediation triangle, this "equilateral" position between the spouses assists the couple to view themselves individually and relationally with greater clarity and objectively. In forming this *conciliation triangle*, the conciliator can help to minimize the complexities created by central and interlocking triangles through focusing on the central concerns between them.

In truth, this is easier said than done and requires a conciliator with a moderately high level of emotional maturity of her own; a fairly low level of chronic anxiety and emotional reactivity; the capacity to remain reasonably calm and objective in an intense situation by seeing system's dynamics; and the ability to view the conciliation as an opportunity for discovery instead of trying to enforce and impose her will on the couple.

A conciliator's systemic assessment is essential for both the wife and the husband and is crucial to their future functioning, regardless of their ultimate decision to reconcile or divorce.

THE SIX-STAGE MARITAL CONCILIATION PROCESS USING BOWEN THEORY

When I began conducting conciliations through the Superior Court of Arizona in Yavapai County, I was allotted two hours for each couple. Recently, however, the court has relaxed the two-hour provision, granting me more latitude to experiment with the length of marital conciliation sessions. At this point, I work with couples for up to four hours in order to complete a comprehensive assessment and consultation.

Greater time flexibility has radically increased the efficacy of my conciliations as anxious and agitated couples now have more time to compose themselves and concentrate on the matters at hand. The two-hour framework created a "one size fits all" structure that limited my effectiveness as a conciliator. Most couples enter conciliation in attack and defend mode, replicating the difficult challenges in their relationship. Two hours did not always provide enough time to develop rapport, calm the system, and shift their focus from other to self. For some couples, even four hours cannot begin to move beyond the relationship damage self-inflicted over the years. Nonetheless, the expanded format has created an opportunity for many couples to push past their entrenched attack and defend structure and experience a more positive outcome to their marital conflicts.

At this point in the evolution of my marital conciliation model, I have expanded my timeframe, while using the structure of a six-stage model. The six stages are organized as follows:

Stage I: Introduction (approximately 10–20 minutes)

During Stage I, I welcome the couple, introduce myself, and have the couple introduce themselves. I discuss the process and stages of conciliation, review confidentiality and ground rules/guidelines, and answer any questions that they may have. I inform the couple that my role is to help them decide whether or not to reconcile and not to impose my beliefs about the appropriateness of staying married. During this introductory phase, I highlight my role as expert consultant to inform them that my experiences as conciliator, mediator, marital therapist, and family psychologist may offer them a different perspective about themselves and their relationship than the one that they currently hold.

Stage II: Overview (approximately 40–60 minutes)

During Stage II, I ask each person to explain what has led to the dissolution proceedings and this conciliation meeting. I explain that I need to learn about them in order to help them. It is usually best to keep this request open so that each person can present the background information and perspective as she and he see fit. As with mediation, it is important to allow each person uninterrupted time to tell his and her story. I am interested in a historical narrative of the relationship, from initial meeting and courtship through current circumstances. Also, like mediation, I manage initial reactivity by prompting each through focused questioning but by minimizing interruptions. The two primary goals of this stage are initial assessment of each person and the relationship system, as well as developing rapport and a balanced working relationship with both husband and wife. It is important to be constantly aware of the level of emotional reactivity. Similar to mediation, it is common for each person to try to triangulate me into the inside position of the triangle with the respective spouse on the outside position of the triangle. While this strategy is ultimately self-defeating, it is automatic, and I avoid becoming triangled by balancing rapport building with each spouse without alienating the other partner.

It is also important to remain conscious of amygdala hyper-arousal. Activation of fight-flight reactions bypasses a person's capacity for thoughtfulness. Evidence of hyper-arousal includes frequent interruptions, angry outbursts, and significant withdrawal reactions. Should I observe any of these indications, I assess if an early caucus is needed to establish or re-establish rapport and to help soothe husband and wife.

Stage III: Caucus (approximately 30–45 minutes)

Unlike mediation where the caucus is optional for many mediators, in my conciliation model, the caucus is essential. There are two crucial and overlapping goals of the caucus. The first goal is to further strengthen the working relationship with the husband and wife in order to help legitimize my position as expert consultant. Rapport building continues, as does hypothesis-testing to help determine both the strengths in the system, individually and collectively, as well as each person's dominant mode of automatically reacting in the relationship. With a strong conciliation triangle established, I can move to the second and more important goal. It is during the caucus that I explore interests, help each person move away from intractable positions, and plant seeds for individual change as I emphasize personal accountability, regardless of whether or not the relationship continues. It is here that I underscore the significance of personal responsibility, self-management, self-definition, and shifting from other-focus to self-focus.

I discuss other systems ideas as they are relevant, such as the person least involved in the relationship having the most power. I point out ineffective patterns, replicated in the conciliation session, which created and perpetuate the current emotional gridlock. I separately coach husband and wife to respond to the other through clarifying personal goals, stating interests, and defining a bottom line as to what is and what is not acceptable in the relationship. This systemic coaching also helps individuals move from criticizing, other-focused accusations to clearer, self-focused statements of interest and personal responsibility.

While caucus meetings are confidential, I encourage information sharing in the re-convened session if I believe that disclosing specific facts or perceptions are important for progress. Similar to a mediation caucus, I balance the time spent with each spouse to avoid becoming triangulated into the relationship. I also use conciliation caucuses for making specific referrals, determining issues of safety, re-balancing power, and other conventional uses established by mediators.

Stage IV: The Exchange (45–60 minutes)

After the caucus, the couple re-convenes for the exchange. During this part of the conciliation, the husband and wife discuss the possibility of reconciliation. I reinforce initial coaching during the caucus as they discuss the status of their marriage with a new perspective and direction. I assist the couple with this discussion, and help them concentrate on making self-responsibility statements, which define what it is that each of them wants. I help loosen entrenched positions so that they can explore what their interests are for themselves individually and in the relationship. Usually, if the couple can encounter some movement in these discussions, that is, if they can begin to experience a different interactional and emotional pattern *and* if one spouse has not emotionally closed down and is only at the conciliation meeting because of a judge's order, the couple may begin to uncover some hope where no hope existed before. Sometimes a softening occurs that allows the spouses to re-experience deep feelings of love and connection.

Stage V: Consultant's Assessment (approximately 20–30 minutes)

During Stage V, I review, refine, and reinforce my assessment of each individual's strengths, dominant interactional style, personal issues, and relationship challenges. I avoid giving an opinion as to whether or not the marriage should continue or dissolve. It is also essential that I not frame the decision simply as a decision to stay or not stay in the marriage but, rather, as a decision to accept personal responsibility for one's own life. In other words, regardless of outcome, my assessment highlights what I have observed and what will lead to more effective personal functioning in general as well as relationship functioning in particular. I help the couple consider that fleeing the marriage will not end their personal difficulties.

Moving a couple from other-focus to self-focus can take months or years depending on the couple's level of basic differentiation, so making this shift in a two to four hour conciliation is not simple. The key variables in facilitating this shift are the differentiation level of the couple, as well as the differentiation level and thus objectivity of the conciliator.

As discussed earlier, one essential feature in maintaining a more differentiated and thus de-triangled stance as a conciliator is establishing a conciliation triangle. In a conciliation triangle, I enter the marital system without absorbing their anxiety. Instead, like an emotional mirror, I reflect back their anxiety, while remaining authentically connected with them and fully committed to the process. While I experience as much failure as success in helping couples make this shift to interests and self-focus, through the conciliation triangle I help couples individually and together experience something different from their old, established, and rigidly conflictual patterns. Even when the spouses reject the option for reconciliation, strengthening individuals through re-aligning this concentration on personal responsibility can go a long way towards promoting emotional maturity in one or both spouses. In this way, future relationships and future life functioning are healthier and a continued relationship with the ex-spouse, if there are children involved, can be less disruptive for the children and the parents.

Stage VI: Decision (approximately 10–20 minutes)

By now, it is almost always clear whether or not the husband and wife want to reconcile. The decision is usually not difficult. They have explored key relationship issues and themes, they have attempted a different interactional style based on accepting more personal responsibility and self-focus, and I have articulated the individual and relationship challenges they must overcome in order for reconciliation to succeed. If the couple decides to reconcile, I offer community referrals for marital therapy. Timely follow-up to the conciliation session helps prevent relapse into non-functional patterns.

I never work with the couple after the conciliation. Self-referring to one's own private practice is an unethical conflict of interest and may undercut the conciliation process itself. Also, having court-referred conciliation couples available for private referral may negatively affect the conciliator's objectivity in the consultant's role.

THREE CASE EXAMPLES

To illustrate the challenges and possibilities of marital conciliations, I will discuss three cases that highlight this model and demonstrate the use of Bowen theory to guide the practice of conciliations.

Anxiety Cascade: Biological Imperatives that Override Conciliation

Early in my work as a conciliator, before I had established my own model of marital conciliation, I was assigned a court-referred couple named Doris and Brian. The spouses had been separated for six months, and Doris requested conciliation. Through her own therapy, Doris said that she had worked on her own issues, and she now wanted to reconcile.

When the session began, however, Doris launched into a tirade of complaints about Brian, blaming him for everything that was wrong with the marriage. He, in turn, reciprocated, blaming Doris for her inability to demonstrate love and affection. Brian was clear that he was attending the session because of a court order and not because he wanted reconciliation. I tried to gain control of the session by having each person speak individually, preventing the non-speaking spouse from interrupting, asking them to write down any responses, etc. These are all traditional skills employed early in a mediation session. Doris was unable to remain silent, despite my urging. After a few minutes of trying to listen to her husband, she stood up and marched out of the conciliation, saying that she could no longer listen to his lies. Doris was gone.

As I reflected on this conciliation, it became obvious that I had erred in conducting the session. What happened was that Doris began experiencing hyper-arousal. Her amygdala had activated. Once this happened, her cortical thinking processes were overloaded and bypassed, and she was left in a state of fight-flight hyper-arousal. When I blocked her attempts to fight with Brian, the only survival reaction left to her was to flee, which she did. Doris was experiencing an anxiety cascade, and her body and mind called for an immediate response to alleviate her perceived threat.

I learned a valuable lesson from this meeting. Couples enter conciliation with their emotions charged and their thinking often affected by their strong feelings. This condition can lead to a survival response that is overwhelming, resulting in automatic hyper-arousal in the form of fight-flight. I learned that it is it is imperative to track emotional escalation in conciliation sessions. Once activated, the amygdala needs time to calm down and return control to the more rational, cortical thinking centers of the brain. Self-soothing becomes crucial and the conciliator can help compose the person by providing a safe, quiet environment.

An early caucus is sometimes essential, providing the time and place to re-group, breathe, and calm down. The conciliator can support this process. If suitable, finding opportunities to experience laughter can aid greatly as appropriate humor can activate other, less reactive portions of the brain.

Better yet, the conciliator must be conscious of amygdala activation before hyper-arousal sets in. Being observant of the following variables is important: the level of tension in a person; her or his capacity to listen without interrupting and reacting; the effectiveness of initial attempts to develop and maintain rapport; and one's own "gut" intuition regarding a situation. Should the conciliator detect emotional escalation by either party, it is crucial to break the three-way meeting and immediately move into early caucus, beginning with the most emotionally reactive party.

In subsequent sessions with other couples, I have effectively managed hyper-arousal using this strategy. Once in caucus, I work to calm the individual, strengthen rapport, and help the husband and wife determine whether or not conciliation is appropriate at this time. Sometimes, mitigating circumstances heighten the person's base level of reactivity, making conciliation more difficult. In one instance, the wife had recently lost her job and was living with her mother. That relationship was very strained. We re-scheduled the conciliation after she developed stability with her own home and a new job. When her life circumstance settled, conciliation was timelier and thus more effective.

It is also important that the conciliator recognize when conciliation is not appropriate. For example, I worked with a man with a severe bi-polar (manic-depressive) disorder, and he was actively psychotic in conciliation. In this state, he was unable to function effectively on his own behalf. He declared that if his wife and he were not going to reconcile, he wanted joint legal and physical custody of their son. During caucus, we discussed the present value of conciliation and I told him that, in my opinion, what he needed was psychiatric treatment and a family law attorney to help advocate for him. I subsequently dismissed the couple from conciliation, informing the court that, in this instance, conciliation was not appropriate.

The Cybersex Triangle

This couple was court-referred based on the wife's request for conciliation. They had been married for three years. Martha was in her early seventies, having been previously divorced for twenty years. Jim was in his mid-sixties and wanted a divorce because he said that their interests had changed and that there was no longer any passion in the marriage. Jim had been married several times in the past, having established a pattern of leaving first. It was clear from the outset that Jim was only in conciliation because of a court order. Nonetheless, I conducted the conciliation using the guidelines outlined previously.

Though Martha had been alone and independent for many years, it was clear from the meeting that she was hoping to "grow old" with Jim and spend the rest of her life with him. Jim, on the other hand, stated that they used to hike and fly airplanes together, and that they had led a very active lifestyle. Jim complained that life with Martha was now too dull, and he was not prepared to lead a sedentary life in his later years. During the overview stage, Martha and Jim interrupted each other constantly, and Martha reiterated her litany of complaints against Jim. It was clear that Jim had heard these complaints before. Martha was especially critical of Jim's cybersex life, as he spent countless hours on the Internet, downloading pornography and excluding her from his sex life. I tried to keep them focused on narrating their own stories as best as I could.

During the individual caucus with Jim, it became clear that he had no interest in salvaging the marriage. He was content with his Internet sex life and claimed that masturbating to pornography provided more variety than did sex with his wife. I assessed Jim's interest in pornography as compulsive and tried to have him focus on improving his relationship with himself and on aspects of his life that he could manage without resorting to his cybersex addiction. I was not successful in de-triangling cybersex from the couple's life.

I had more success with Martha during her individual caucus. I asked her if their patterned interaction as a couple was similar to what I observed in conciliation. She acknowledged that it was the same, with Martha pushing Jim to give up cybersex and return to her. She spoke about how, as a woman in her seventies, she could not compete with the physicality of the Internet women and expressed despair, frustration, and anger about even having to try to measure up to these women. I asked her if she was willing to risk trying something different when we reconvened. She stated that she was, as she had nothing to lose at this point. I coached her to self-focus on both what she wanted from the relationship and what she wanted for her own emotional well being rather than focusing on changing Jim. Perhaps out of desperation, she embraced my perspective and decided to try something different. I coached her to use I language, focusing on stating her personal desires and dreams, as well as soothing herself, regardless of Jim's reactions. In effect, I helped Martha to self-soothe, think, and act differently.

When we re-convened, Jim made it clear that he liked his life the way it was, that he wanted a more active lifestyle than Martha afforded him, and that he was perfectly content with his daily and extended cybersex routine. Martha focused on herself, stating what she wanted from the relationship and in her life. She made it clear that she wanted to remain married to Jim. She did a remarkable job of remaining calm and using I language.

In the end, Jim refused her offer to reconcile and left the meeting unchanged. Martha, on the other hand, encountered a profound emotional shift. She told me that she had experienced a strength she had not known in years, and she was committed to re-discovering her own life goals and not being defined by how Jim saw her. She cried over the loss of the marriage and asked me for a reassuring hug, which I willingly provided. I believe that her new determination came from a spark of self-definition and her willingness to begin managing her own life without Jim. I referred her to Harriet Lerner's (1989) outstanding book on marriage and family relationships, *The Dance of Intimacy*, which is an important resource for women that uses Bowen theory as its framework. In this case example, I believe that the conciliation, while not repairing the marriage, provided a foundation and framework for Martha's developing emotional maturity.

Fundamentalism and Emotional Reactivity

This couple was court-referred based on the wife's request for conciliation. Luke and Susan were members of a fundamentalist church and had a very set, structured view of the husband being the head of the household and the wife being subservient to the husband. Though Susan filed for both marital dissolution and conciliation, Luke willingly participated. The presenting problems were two-fold. First, Susan accused Luke of cheating on her by looking at other women with "lust in his heart." According to her and quoting biblical scripture, looking at other women was tantamount to infidelity and reflected his impure heart and a battle with the devil for his soul. Luke, for his part, had left the home because of escalating tension and his increased frustration threatened to erupt into violence. His anger and capacity for violence against his wife frightened him. Separating was his attempt to regulate their closeness and thus diminish the possibility of his becoming violent. According to Susan, if they were not living together they were breaking their marriage vows.

On the surface, Susan appeared less differentiated. She triangulated biblical scripture to reinforce her positions and used church teachings to strengthen her statements. Susan seemed less mature in her emotional make-up and was limited in her ability to respond through thoughtful discussions and an objective understanding of their situation. Understanding Bowen theory helped me view Luke's relative calm and clarity in creating safety through distance and Susan's reactive attempts to bring him back to the marriage through pursuing, even at the cost of her possible safety, as two sides of the same "differentiation coin." Luke came from a physically abusive home, and he carried a great deal of anger. He used religion as a way of trying to manage his anger but the conflict with his wife quickly brought that rage to the surface. Luke's distance and his reliance on his own biblical interpretations to justify his actions reflected the same limited emotional development as Susan's pursuing. In other words, the couple shared a similar level of basic differentiation, even though on the surface the husband appeared more functional and the wife appeared less functional. They were engaged in the process of borrowing and trading of selves in the marriage. My initial assessment was characteristic of most couples in conciliation: each used "you language" to articulate what the other had done to create and exacerbate the problems in the marriage; each blamed the other for the failing marriage; and each proposed solutions to their difficulties based on how the other needed to change.

Under these emotional conditions, I caucused with them separately. Meeting individually was extraordinarily effective in calming the system. By providing a more differentiated presence—remaining calm and deepening my rapport individually with Luke and Susan—I begin to shift their focus from blaming to assuming greater personal responsibility and self-development. In effect, I supported each spouse's efforts to clarify what it was that each wanted, including Susan's "bottom line" that she would not wait forever for Luke to return to their marriage and live together, as well as the Luke's desire to not re-enter the marriage while the threat of violence was alive for him.

To help de-triangulate the Bible, church elders, and her parents, I asked each of them separately what they wanted, what they were willing to do in response to the other, and what parts of their individual and marital lives were non-negotiable. During this process, I helped them remain available to each other and not automatically distance or pursue out of anxiety.

Susan became aware that she had no power regarding her husband's separation, and that, in fact, as the person least involved in the marriage Luke had the most power. As such, I coached Susan to define her personal goals and her goals for the marriage. Susan became clear about several concerns and several interests. First, she decided that their weekends together (the husband was at this point working out of town and they only had weekends together) would not include sexual intimacy. Susan felt strongly that sexual intimacy should be reserved for marriage and she defined marriage, in part, as living and working together to make the relationship work. Susan increased her confidence and clarity as she realized that, while she did not have any power over Luke's need for physical separation, she could control her responses to his weekend sexual advances and not undercut her self-esteem by satisfying them. Susan realized the importance of giving her husband some time to figure out whether or not he was going to return, though she set a "bottom line" timetable of six months, after which she would re-institute divorce proceedings.

Luke also responded well. (Respect for authority is an important component of most fundamentalist churches and, as such, I believe that the couple responded well to my position as a representative of the Superior Court and my extensive experience as a family psychologist, marriage and family therapist, mediator, and conciliator.) Luke realized that the most important issue for him was managing his temper and not putting his wife or himself in danger. I made a referral to an anger management group and stressed the point that regardless of Susan's "provocations," he was solely responsible for his behavior and responses. I suggested that until he felt personally empowered and strong enough to ensure that physical abuse was not a possibility, it was essential that he not return home and thereby create a dangerous situation. I coached Luke in understanding that Susan's position regarding his seeming infidelity, abandonment, and other concerns were all opportunities for him to re-focus on himself and what he needed to do for himself and the marriage. I further coached Luke, as I had coached Susan, that the challenges we identified in caucus were the same challenges that they each faced individually. Whether or not their marriage survived, divorce would not resolve these basic issues of selfhood.

When we reconvened for Stage IV, "the exchange," I highlighted their strengths, including their commitment to their marriage. I coached the couple to communicate using I language and to gain as much clarity as possible as to why their marriage was important to them individually, collectively, and religiously. I called on them to state what each was willing to do to repair their marriage and helped them clarify to each other what their respective "bottom lines" were. The caucus meetings had helped quiet the system and allowed for progress in these areas.

In Stage V, "consultant's assessment," I applauded Susan and Luke's efforts to communicate differently and to accept more personal responsibility;

I carefully reiterated the individual and relationship strengths and challenges; and I reinforced that whether or not they decided to reconcile, the issues we were discussing still pertained to their functioning as individuals.

During Stage VI, "decision," Susan and Luke decided that, based on their religious conviction and their love for each other, they owed it to themselves and each other to attempt marital reconciliation. I referred them to a church elder with whom they each felt comfortable, as well as to a secular marital therapist in the community.

In the end, my attempt to calm the system by providing a more differentiated presence helped shift the emotional atmosphere for the couple, thus enabling them to gain a measure of clarity about themselves as individuals and their relationship. In addition, the reactivity of the active triangles was reduced enough for them to try a new way of communicating. They were able to present themselves directly to one another without the complications brought on by escalating anxiety in the central and interlocking triangles.

Conducting a marital conciliation is always challenging. It is a court-ordered, last attempt to salvage a battered marriage. Often, one person is only attending because of the court order. Sometimes, spousal abuse is present and safety issues override the importance of this court-mandated session. While demanding and sometimes frustrating, I find conciliations a fascinating opportunity to help couples find a productive path in their lives, individually and, sometimes, collectively. Working with this six-stage model, and having a theoretical framework based on Bowen theory to guide me, I am discovering opportunities for success that were not available to me previously.

Over the years I have modified my approach to conciliations. In addition to providing increased flexibility relating to time, I only conduct conciliations when the husband and wife are both willing to participate. While a judge can order couples to attend conciliation, once in attendance, I find that voluntary participation follows an important ethical guideline present in mediation, that of self-determination. Also, the court now actively screens cases for domestic violence, and, if present, we are careful to separate husbands and wives to different waiting areas. While I have worked with a number of couples where a history of domestic violence exists, voluntary participation is essential, and these cases are carefully managed to insure safety.

To date, my conciliation success rate is approximately 50% for those who choose voluntary participation, with success defined as the couple agreeing to marital reconciliation and withdrawing their dissolution petition. As a family psychologist and conciliator, however, I do not determine success from these criteria alone. First, while successful conciliations help unclog the overburdened courts, they do not necessarily result in successful marriages. Marital success can only be judged over time, through committed work and sustained efforts. Currently, there is no mechanism to track these marriages in the court system. Second, living in a relatively small town, there are limited opportunities to make referrals to marriage specialists, especially those subscribing to a systems perspective. As such, I sometimes question whether the work that I accomplish in creating clarity and hope is sustained or whether it all falls apart weeks or months later through ineffective marriage therapy or a lack of follow-through on the couple's part.

Yet, more hopefully, I see myself as a gardener, tilling the soil, planting seeds for change, and giving people a different perspective on how they can grow as individuals and in intimate relationships. I often provide books and articles to encourage spouses to continue their emotional development, and I emphasize that the work done within marriage can often accelerate the emotional maturation process more quickly than does the dissolution of the marriage. While I am not there to witness which seeds germinate and flourish and which do not, I believe that the conciliation opportunity provided by the courts can spur individuals to take more responsibility for their lives and towards their children, and that a Bowen family systems theory approach helps me become a more effective gardener.

I use marital conciliation meetings to encourage couples, individually and together, to seek out solutions to their complex problems through thoughtful dialogue, commitment, and perseverance, seeing divorce as an option never to be taken lightly and only as a last resort. Guided by Bowen theory, with a six-stage model, marital conciliations offer the last, best hope for couples seeking a final opportunity to heal the wounds in their marriage through increasing their emotional maturity.

The following chapter extends the application of Bowen theory to training and supervising mediators.

Part III

A NEW MODEL OF
MEDIATION TRAINING

Chapter Eleven

Training and Supervising Mediators Using Bowen Theory

One of the advantages of "seeing systems" and applying Bowen theory to human interactions is that this understanding of the world is not limited to a precise way of operating in a particular discipline or activity. The universality of Bowen theory to all human interactions, if not all biotic systems, suggests that it is equally valid and pragmatic for training and supervising mediators as well as conducting mediations. As such, I use Bowen theory to train and supervise mediators as a senior mediator and trainer at the Yavapai County Superior Court in Arizona and as a Professor of Peace Studies and Psychology at Prescott College. I have also conducted state and national workshops applying Bowen theory to mediation.

As such, I find Bowen theory a valuable model in training and supervising new mediators and providing professional development opportunities for seasoned mediators. In truth, most students and professionals who are exposed to Bowen theory find it intellectually stimulating as well as eminently pragmatic. Those who commit to mediating systemically also find themselves "thinking systems" in other areas of their work and personal lives. Bowen theory has a way of saturating an adherent's world in ways that other theories of human functioning rarely do. This chapter explores the use of Bowen theory to instruct, train, and supervise new mediators as well as to coach experienced professionals. I will discuss how the theory and training are presented to both groups and how learning and teaching through an active pedagogy is consistent with Bowen theory, resulting in more effective training and teaching.

FOUNDATIONS OF TRAINING

As part of my educational responsibilities at Prescott College, I have developed and teach a number of courses that introduce and apply Bowen theory to a variety of micro-systems and macro-systems. These include: *Counseling Theories, Family Systems Theory, Family Systems in Film and Literature, Models of Leadership: Leadership through Differentiation, American Government: Politics, Power, & the Enlightenment Vision, Social Psychology: The Meaning of Contemporary Events, Community Mediation and Principled Negotiation* and *Advanced Mediation Practicum.* Classes such as *Counseling Skills* and *Family Systems Theory* introduce Bowen theory as a way of understanding individual and family behavior. In essence, these are more micro-systemic applications of the theory and are consistent with the original intentions of Murray Bowen when he developed his theory to treat individuals and families. *Family Systems in Film and Literature* is an interdisciplinary class, co-taught with K.L. Cook, a professional writer and literature professor, which examines how Bowen theory concepts seem intuitively understood by the best writers and filmmakers through their work. We examine the structure and function of the family through films, plays, novels, novellas, and short stories, and how the works of imaginative writers and filmmakers are consistent with the tenets of Bowen theory. We have documented the structure and content of this course elsewhere (Cook and Regina, 2006).

American Government: Politics, Power, & the Enlightenment Vision is a second interdisciplinary class and examines the intersection of political theory and systems theory at a macro-systemic level. Here, Bowen theory is used to comprehend "the body politic," political leaders, and political leadership as well as societal emotional process, a Bowen theory macro-systemic concept that explores societal emotional progression and societal emotional regression, and their interrelationship with other Bowen theory concepts. *Social Psychology: The Meaning of Contemporary Events* investigates Bowen theory and social psychology, and their applications to macro-level events both nationally and internationally. The basis of this course includes exploring societal triangulation, societal chronic anxiety and reactivity, differentiating within highly emotional social environments, as well as examining the intersection between systems thinking and social psychology.

Models of Leadership: Leadership through Differentiation combines both the micro-systemic and macro-systemic applications of Bowen theory by examining what makes for effective leadership, exploring the personal biographies of differentiated leaders such as Abraham Lincoln, Elizabeth Cady Stanton, Susan B. Anthony, Ernest Shackleton, and Queen Elizabeth I, and applying the concept of differentiated leadership to organizations, businesses, and politics. Finally, *Community Mediation and Principled Negotiation* and *Advanced Mediation Practicum* directly apply Bowen theory for students interested in learning mediation and becoming certified mediators. Here, we also explore the interaction of Bowen theory with principled negotiation, a model of conflict resolution first proposed by Roger Fisher and William Ury (1981) in *Getting to Yes*.

Research on effective education indicates that learning is social and that people learn best by doing. At its heart, Bowen theory provides a natural link with effective mediation training strategies as it integrates current research in brain-based learning with active and challenging learning environments, a dynamic pedagogy, and opportunities for reflection and review.

As I have asserted throughout the book, the core of Bowen theory lies in the central concept of differentiation, which is the individuality and together-ness life forces in action. Higher differentiation levels are viewed as crucial to effective learning and living. That is, success in developing and strengthening differentiation levels significantly influences content and process learning. Managing oneself responsibly in highly ambiguous and anxious situations, the capacity to hear, offer, and integrate support and feedback, and the ability to incorporate public debrief and reflection are all aptitudes associated with higher levels of emotional maturity.

They are also the same qualities essential for effective mediators and for effective mediator training. By strengthening differentiation, the more emo-tionally mature individual becomes a more capable and ready learner and, ultimately, a more proficient mediator. And, perhaps most significantly, the differentiation level of the educator and trainer, as leader of the classroom or educational setting, is the single most important influence on the educational environment of which the learners are a part. In other words, learning envi-ronments that encourage development of differentiation are best promoted by educators who themselves are dedicated to enhancing their own emotional maturity. This is especially true for educators and students involved in me-diation training. As I discussed in Chapter 5, "Emotional Maturity and the Mediator," the most successful mediators are those with the greatest capacity to self-define, self-manage, connect deeply and compassionately with others, and maintain humor, passionate engagement, and non-attachment to outcome.

Mediation training programs using Bowen theory as a guide thus have two parallel but interconnected goals: (1) skill development in the essential com-ponents of mediation—learning the stages of mediation, reframing, moving from positions to interests, exploring BATNAs and WATNAs, B SMART agreement writing, etc.—and (2) increasing the differentiation levels of the trainees. Utilizing learned skills without a moderately to highly differenti-ated presence are likely to render the mediator too vulnerable to emotional reactivity and thus generate ineffectual mediations. Moderately to highly differentiated mediators without appropriate skill sets are likewise apt to render the mediation ineffective since mediators must not only know themselves and how to responsibly manage themselves and others but also be capable of understanding and applying the pragmatics of the mediation process itself. To accomplish these goals, I developed an 11-week course, *Community Mediation and Principled Negotiation*, which helps students enhance their differentiation capacities, learn Bowen theory and develop new mediation skills. In the second course, *Advanced Mediation Practicum,* students follow up their basic training with more advanced training, applying their theory and skills to actual mediations.

COLLEGE TRAINING AND SUPERVISION

As is consistent with most mediation training programs, an essential component of these courses centers on skill development and lively pedagogical activities designed to learn and refine proficiency. Through modeling, guided practice, and application, students develop increased capacities in listening, reflecting, rapport-building, reframing, shifting from positions to interests, and agreement writing. While effective mediation training programs all use modeling and mediation role plays as the core of training, supervision, and skill development, the essential difference with a training program based on Bowen theory as a guiding foundation is that these activities are all framed and executed around understanding and applying Bowen theory to the mediation itself—managing disputants, developing mediation triangles, using caucus to increase functional differentiation in the disputants, etc.—as well as encouraging an understanding of self and others through promoting increased differentiation levels in the trainees. The hands-on, skills observation and enhancement components are supplemented by various readings, discussions, and activities designed to develop an understanding of Bowen theory, commit to the principles of the theory, and use the theory as a guide in training and supervision. While eschewing mediation training as personal therapy, students, nonetheless, come to understand themselves—their strengths, weaknesses, personal sensitivities around issues and feelings, and individual emotional triggers—in ways that advance their own emotional maturity in order to become more effective novice mediators.

Secondly, and perhaps just as importantly, as a Bowen theory practitioner and trainer, I put myself in learning situations that challenge me. It is my hope that, as the educational leader, if I can become a more differentiated presence in the classroom, this will promote an emotional field or atmosphere that will support learning and risk-taking by the students.

In fact, Friedman (1987, 2007) and Goleman (2006) suggest that leaders in any human system are the most influential individuals in creating the emotional field in which learning and leading occur. If leaders in educational environments are capable of promoting a "positive resonance" or differentiated presence such that they are viewed as equal partners in learning, while maintaining their position of leaders in the system, then classroom and other educational environments can be more readily transformed into communities where learning is better supported throughout the educational setting (Boyatzis, 2002). In other words, a leader with a moderate to high level of emotional maturity who is committed to developing her differentiation capacity is a more competent and effective leader and thus trainer. As a leader, the more emotionally mature the teacher is, the greater his capacity to promote differentiation in the educational endeavor. For Bowen (2002), Friedman (2007) and others (Goldman, Boyatzis, & McKee, 2002), this is the most important variable in successful learning and leading. Who among us has not experienced this firsthand, where the self-responsible, non-defensive educator with a high capacity to engage others creates the dynamic conditions for learning, while the less emotionally mature leader fails regardless of the sophistication of the lesson plan?

As the instructor, I want to set the emotional tone for risk-taking, learning from students, and accepting their feedback, since they will receive mine throughout the courses. For the class *Community Mediation and Principled Negotiation*, I accomplish this through two mediation role-play demonstrations. For each mock mediation, two student volunteers create the conflict scenario and role-play the parts of disputants. I then demonstrate the stages of mediation through a "stop-and-go" process whereby each stage is de-briefed with the entire class before proceeding to the next stage. At the end of each role-play mediation, the entire activity is debriefed from both personal and theoretical perspectives.

These two class exercises are particularly important in developing a class culture promoting differentiation. They are examples of my actively participating in dynamic pedagogical activities where I expose myself to the same scrutiny and risk-taking that I expect students to expose themselves to throughout the course and the training. As the instructor, I enter the role play mediations with a substantial degree of uncertainty about the process and outcome. I conduct the mediations and solicit public feedback, support, and critique from the students. All the while, I am providing a forum for students to learn how to give and receive feedback, and promoting my own differentiation as I manage my performance anxiety, develop rapport with the participants, define and clarify roles and guidelines for the mediation, and provide a template for conducting community mediations. I help set a resonant emotional tone for the learning environment through my willingness to be an active and responsible co-learner in the educational process through these and other pedagogically active class lessons.

Mediator training is an extensive process that begins with the initial class session and progresses through a carefully planned and executed scope and sequence. Using the introductory course as a case in point, I will use several examples of this developmental process to highlight my approach.

During the first class meeting, students share why they are interested in becoming mediators. This structured activity is designed to begin the process of developing a sense of personal ownership for the course and its success. It provides students with the opportunity to reflect on their personal interests and goals, as well as to engage with others to formulate a common vision. This activity also provides me an opportunity to assess each class participant's level of emotional maturity. Within the boundaries of the course description, the students and I co-create the learning goals that we will address during the semester. The students are asked to brainstorm specific skills and theories they want to cover. Topics are added and subtracted from the developing list until a consensus is reached. In its final form, the topics generated commonly include an understanding of conflict and conflict resolution, acquiring mediation skills, and improving interpersonal communication proficiency.

Through this exercise, students begin the process of developing personal and collective responsibility for the class. They help formulate course topics and goals, and by so doing, they define the course for themselves, manage their own emotional reactivity to the interests and goals of others, and work cooperatively and collectively to take others' interests into consideration. This initial undertaking is specifically designed to help students clarify their expectations and sets the stage for what is expected throughout the training.

Next, students are asked what attitudes and behaviors we should expect from each other in order to successfully achieve our educational goals. This "group norming" exercise in developing clear and shared expectations, as well as common agreements, is critical to the success of the group as a learning community. Trainee responses usually include: say what you need, help others, have fun, actively participate, respect self and others, maintain confidentiality, take risks, arrive on time, be prepared for class, and so on. The students and I then commit to these common agreements and sign a group contract to hold each other accountable. The symbolic gesture of signing the agreement signifies commitment. If a participant breaks an agreement later in the training, the group as a whole is asked to respond to the transgression using the spirit of the contract as a rubric. This continues the process of creating a sense of group responsibility for the success of the course. In addition, this exercise asks students to take personal and collective responsibility for their actions throughout the course, thus further promoting self-differentiation.

In a second example designed to assess and interpret how students view and manage conflict, students are paired together and given a small cup of M&Ms. They were told the following: "You are going to play a fun game of arm wrestling. The winner of each arm wrestling contest can eat one M&M. Please play until all the M&Ms are eaten."

During the activity, much laughter ensues as trainees begin competing. After a brief period of time, many of the pairs discover that if they cooperate they can share the M&Ms by taking turns winning. The activity is debriefed around the concepts of cooperation, competition, and conflict. Students are asked to reflect on how they managed the activity, the level of conflict and cooperation they created, and their degree of anxiety and comfort around competition. Through the de-briefing process, the students discuss what they learned about themselves regarding the central topics.

In other activities, which occur throughout the term, students learn the specific skills of mediation. While the personal and interpersonal capacities of the students provide the theoretical "vehicle" for traveling down the road of skill development and improvement, students are required to master a set of specific mediation stages and skills along the way in order to successfully complete the training. These stages and skills, as outlined in Chapter 3, "Applying Bowen Theory to the Six-Stage Model of Mediation," are introduced in sequence and include:

- Stage 1-Introductions: Review; writing and practicing introductions
- Stage 2-Uninterrupted Time: Personal Narratives; review and practice
- Stage 3-The Exchange: Developing Connections; review and practice
- Stage 4-Developing Options: Brainstorming & Refining Options; review and practice
- Stage 5-Writing the Agreement: B SMART Agreements; review and practice
- Stage 6-Closing: Summing up, managing disputants who are not successful in formulating a common agreement

Developing specific skills for implementing each stage follow a consistent pattern. First, students read about the stage. Next, I present the micro-skills for each stage either through demonstrations or through examples that are discussed and processed. Finally, students practice each stage and specific skill through sample vignette mediations. As students develop the skills necessary for each stage, the subsequent stage is layered on, so that students learn the sequence of mediation as well as the skill set required to successfully implement each skill and each stage. Students rotate through the roles of disputants and co-mediators so that each student experiences every role in the mediation process. Throughout the training, I observe each mediation group and provide critique and feedback to the participants. As necessary, I insert myself into the mediation process as co-mediator to re-direct a mediation that has lost its focus, to demonstrate a particular technique or skill, or to prompt the mediators into examining issues and interests that they may have missed.

By integrating a variety of active learning exercises and skill development scenarios throughout the course, I try to foster and develop emotional maturity in trainees through a feedback loop by presenting the material, discussing the stages and skills for the lesson, implementing the activity through role plays, providing individual feedback, and de-briefing with the entire class. As students progress through the stages, new vignettes are introduced to keep the mediation role-plays fresh and to give students an opportunity to implement entire practice mediations. Perhaps most importantly, I expose trainees to a variety of challenging situations that allow them to gauge their own capacities, monitor their own performances, reflect on situations that activate emotional reactions, and promote more effective management of challenging mediation situations.

Students learn through structured environments with highly uncertain outcomes. They need the personal strength to develop and implement new skills in a public arena where they are critiqued by other students and by the instructor. I am continually inspired by the courage that students display throughout the learning process. They realize that the best way for them to learn is through an active, ordered pedagogy that provides opportunities to directly experience and thus learn the material; to take risks in emotionally safe environments and through activities that will naturally raise their anxiety levels; and to de-brief their learning in both private venues, such as portfolio reflections, as well as public arenas, such as small group critiques and large group discussions. This process is consistent with my experiences in other courses that I teach, where I employ strategies designed to raise the differentiation level of students.

Through opportunities crafted to increase emotional maturity, students learn about themselves and develop increased capacities to work cooperatively with each other. In doing so, they acquire academic, theoretical knowledge along with specific skills sets useful for accomplishing the goals of the training and transferable to the world outside of the classroom.

Seasoned trainers or mediators may find themselves reflecting that their own training programs or their personal training when they first learned the mediation process were *experientially* similar to the curriculum described that infuses Bowen theory in the mediation training process. In fact, most of us were trained to learn the stages of mediation, apply the skills in role-plays, integrate feedback from trainers, and develop an identity as a professional mediator. The core difference with a training program based on Bowen theory, however, is the commitment of the trainer to promoting emotional maturity in the trainees and framing the entire training environment and the mediation process itself within the context of the theory. With Bowen theory as a guide, the mediation training program has a central focus, a hub around which novice mediation practitioners can evolve into effective professional mediators.

SUPERVISING AND TRAINING EXPERIENCED MEDIATORS

In some ways, training and supervising experienced mediators present more challenges than training and supervising new mediators. Experienced mediators have developed a repertoire of skills and strategies that often entrench them in their work. These skills and strategies sometimes serve them well and sometimes create obstacles to conducting effective mediations. Not surprisingly, the more emotionally mature the experienced mediators are, the more receptive they also are to investigating their effectiveness and exploring ways to increase their abilities. Reciprocally, the lower the self-differentiation of experienced mediators, the more attached they are to their mediation style and approach, and the less receptive they are to meaningfully examining their effectiveness.

Having conducted a number of trainings, supervisions, and workshops with experienced mediators, the majority of seasoned mediators with whom I have worked have positively responded to training and supervision in Bowen theory and practice. Many comment that the theory makes both intuitive and logical sense and that their work already mirrors a Bowen theory approach to conducting mediations. A common response is that Bowen theory presents a useful framework to understand how they work as mediators and a guide to increasing their personal and professional effectiveness. They notice that the theory offers a common language, and that a systems approach to conducting mediations provides a helpful structure for understanding disputants, implementing the stages, and utilizing techniques more effectively.

Central to training and supervising experienced mediators is the effect of the trainer's level of differentiation on the seasoned workshop participants. More highly differentiated trainers effectively promote emotional maturity in educational and training settings. This emotional development of experienced mediators must occur holistically throughout the learning community and through an on-going peer training and peer supervision program. Brief two-to-three hour workshops or even full-day seminars at conferences can stimulate curiosity about Bowen theory and practice, but increasing effectiveness as a Bowen theory mediation practitioner requires a long-term commitment to increasing one's level of basic differentiation and, as such, necessitates consistent effort over extended periods of time. Those seasoned professionals willing to embark on this adventure should not be expected to take risks in isolation. In particular, Bowen theory trainers and supervisors, as educational leaders, must be willing to subject themselves to the same scrutiny and trials as their peers. Educator Thomas Armstrong (1994) reinforces this point when he writes, "Before applying any model of learning…we should first apply it to ourselves as educators and adult learners, for unless we have an experiential understanding of the theory and have personalized its content, we are unlikely to be committed to using it with students" (p. 16).

This practice is central for Bowen theory mediation trainers and supervisors. Trainers and peers alike must be active participants in learning. As a trainer and supervisor, for example, my willingness to "walk my talk" is not simply a matter of fairness and balance. It is, rather, a function of setting an emotional atmosphere and tone in which learning is valued through a challenging environment that engages us all as learners. I ask those being trained and supervised to offer constructive feedback to each other, and I provide opportunities to publicly debrief our own learning challenges so that we, as co-learners, can reflect on our experiences and share what we learn with everyone. The professional boundary between peers and trainer/supervisor is naturally more diffuse than between undergraduate students and instructor. As professionals, we all share common life experiences, joys, and difficulties in our work lives. A peer support system based on Bowen theory allows us to honestly grapple with our challenges and mutually celebrate our successes. Finally, a structured commitment to maturing and learning over time provides a professional network wherein we all grow, learn, and evolve.

In training and supervising peer mediators, I develop training activities that are varied and extensive. For example, we focus on advanced techniques, debrief cases, review the current literature and controversies, and explore any number of topics and approaches. In all instances, however, the activities and discussions are specifically designed to promote differentiation through using Bowen theory to guide our work. In some instances, the training and supervision may be more theoretical or cognitive, at other times the training and supervision may examine a peer mediator's family of origin in an attempt to uncover the emotional block that prevents him from successfully assisting a particular type of disputant. At still other times, I use a demonstration to highlight a particular aspect of the theory. While variety in a long-term peer supervision and training program is essential, "all roads lead to Rome," such that all pedagogical activities, theoretical discussions, and case de-briefings are designed to help increase mediator self-responsibility, self-management, self-capacity, and ability to more effectively connect with others in ways that promote their own emotional maturity as well as to increase disputants' functional differentiation.

Fortunately, I have encountered extraordinary success through integrating personal development with academic and skill-based knowledge acquisition. This approach to education and training includes all of the hallmarks of effective learning through a theoretical system that promotes more differentiated individuality and togetherness as foundational to ongoing success in learning inside and outside of the classroom and training setting. Training and supervising that develops and strengthens emotional maturity is training and supervising that promotes greater personal and professional effectiveness. More emotionally mature people can, in turn, more efficiently integrate and synthesize knowledge and information to become more productive mediators in particular and more effective citizens in general. Active training programs based on Bowen theory, because of their emphasis on action and reflection, are perfect crucibles for increasing integrity and self-capacity. I believe this is one of the primary reasons that a Bowen theory based training program can be professionally and personally life changing.

The final chapter reflects on Bowen theory and its application to mediation and life.

Chapter Twelve

Concluding Thoughts

Those of us who have committed to comprehending and applying Bowen theory in our professional and personal lives continue to appreciate all that the theory has to offer. Murray Bowen began this journey over a half a century ago, and he and others have dedicated innumerable years to strengthening the theory and finding ways to implement it across disciplines and even across species.

I believe that this book adds to this growing body of work by articulating an approach to mediation based on Bowen theory. I began conceptualizing this application of the theory in the early 1990s and published my first article on the subject in the Winter 2000 issue of *Mediation Quarterly*. The response to that article was quite positive and very encouraging, so I set out to more fully elaborate my ideas in this book. Colleagues familiar with Bowen theory expressed excitement after reading drafts of the book. They supported me with suggestions, ideas, and edits, and I persisted through a number of drafts and modifications.

Over the years, I continued to revise my thinking about and my application of the theory through my work as a mediator. For example, I was curious about whether or not different types of mediations—civil, victim-offender, domestic—affected how I implemented Bowen theory. I paired with a number of co-mediators who were learning the theory and observed if their growing comprehension of Bowen theory influenced their effectiveness as mediators. I searched for exceptions to both the theory itself and applying the theory. I examined whether or not working with individuals from diverse backgrounds and demographics influenced the usefulness of the theory in practice. In all instances, it appeared that applying Bowen theory to mediation improved the work of mediators and helped disputants more effectively resolve their differences.

No theory is the absolute truth and all theories are refined or replaced by more accurate theories over time. Attachment to Bowen theory itself can be a form of anxiety binding, so I caution the reader to avoid any zealousness as a Bowen theorist and practitioner. While Bowen theory is a remarkable intellectual and pragmatic theory, it is, after all, a theory, and I warn against confusing this or any theory with reality.

Finally, practitioners of Bowen theory are different in their approaches, since they are different people. Friedman (1991) once asked: how does one differentiate from differentiation? In other words, he recognized that his understanding of Bowen theory is a bit different than Michael Kerr's or Daniel Papero's understanding of the theory. I have likewise observed that different theorist and practitioners of Bowen theory emphasize differing aspects of the theory. In particular, the concept of differentiation is conceptualized slightly differently by the major Bowen theorist writers. There are no absolute truths in how one understands and applies the theory, since, as humans, we are different people trying to make sense of the same material.

Nonetheless, Bowen theory remains a remarkable contribution offered by Murray Bowen to the world. Advocates of Bowen theory are growing in number and, while the vast number of its practitioners remain in the field of marriage and family therapy, over the years and decades, the Annual Symposium at the Bowen Center/Georgetown Family Center in Washington, D.C. has hosted a number of speakers who have applied Bowen theory to disciplines as diverse as zoology, botany, genetics, medicine, and sociobiology. Bowen theory is a theory about evolution and about life, and, as such, humans are a part of the theory and its application.

As we seek to find more and more effective ways to help resolve conflict and promote peace, Bowen theory offers us a powerful tool for creating new and better opportunities for managing differences through self-determination, compassion, fairness, justice, and collaboration. I hope that you, the reader, have found a new personal and professional paradigm for more successful functioning in the world and for acquiring greater wisdom. I assure you that if you continue to learn and apply Bowen theory, over time, your life and those whom you touch will transform for the better. What better gift is there?

References

Adler, P. (1984). The balancing act of mediation training. *Training and Development Journal*, July, 55–58.

Armstrong, T. (1994). *Multiple intelligences in the classroom*. Alexandria, VA: ASCD.

Astor, H. (2007). Mediator neutrality: Making sense of theory and practice. *Social and Legal Studies*, 16 (2), 221–239.

Astor H. and Chinkin, C. (1992). *Dispute resolution in Australia*. Sydney: Butterworths.

Atkinson, B. (1999, July–August). The emotional imperative. *Family Therapy Networker*, 22–33.

Bateson, G., Jackson, D.D., Haley, J., & Weakland, J. (1956). Toward a theory of schizophrenia. *Behavioral Science*, 1, 251–264.

Benjamin, M. and Irving, H.H. (2007). Research in family mediation: Review and implications. *Conflict Resolution Quarterly*, 13 (1), 53–82.

Bethel, C. (1986). The use of separate sessions in family mediation. *Negotiation Journal,* 2(3), 257–271.

Boulle, L. (1996). Mediation: Principles, process, practice. Sydney: Butterworths.

Bowen, M. (1966). The use of family theory in clinical practice. *Comprehensive Psychiatry.* 7, 345–374.

Bowen, M. (1971). Family therapy and family group therapy. In H. Kaplan & B. Sadock (Eds.), *Comprehensive group psychotherapy* (pp. 384–421). Baltimore, MD: Williams & Wilkins.

Bowen, M. (2002). *Family therapy in clinical practice*. Northvale, NJ: Jason Aronson.

Boyatzis, (2002, April 24). Positive resonance: Educational leadership through emotional intelligence. *Education Week*, 52, 40–41.

Buber, M., translated by Smith, R.G. (2000). *I and thou*. New York: Simon and Schuster.

Carter, B. and McGoldrick, M. (1989). Overview: The changing family life-cycle—A framework for family therapy. In B. Carter & M. McGoldrick (Eds.), *The changing family life cycle—A framework for family therapy, second edition* (pp. 3–28), Boston: Allyn and Bacon.

Carter, B. and McGoldrick, M. (2005). *The expanded family life cycle: individual, family and social perspectives, 3rd edition.* Boston, MA: Allyn & Bacon.

Cohen, O., Dattner, N., and Luxenburg, A. (2007). The limits of mediator's neutrality. *Conflict Resolution* Quarterly, 16 (4), 341–348.

Cook, K.L. & Regina, W. (2006). Interdisciplinary team teaching: Family systems in film and literature. In R. D. Johnson (Ed.), *Teachable moments: Essays on experiential education.* Lanham, Maryland: University Press of America, Inc.

Dicks, H.V. (1953). Experiences with marital tensions seen in the psychological clinic. *British Journal of Medical Psychiatry*, 26, 181–196.

Dillow, R. (1996). The school as an emotional system. In P.A. Comella, J. Bader, J.S. Ball, K. Wiseman & R.R. Sagar (Eds.), *The emotional side of organizations: Applications of Bowen theory* (pp. 130–137), Georgetown, MD: Georgetown Family Center.

Ferrera, S.J. (1996). Lessons from nature on leadership. In P.A. Comella, J. Bader, J.S. Ball, K. Wiseman & R.R. Sagar (Eds.), *The emotional side of organizations: Applications of Bowen theory* (pp. 130–137), Georgetown, MD: Georgetown Family Center.

Field, R. (2000). Neutrality and power: Myths and reality. *ADR Bulletin,* 3 (1), May/June 2000, 16–19.

Fisher, R. and Ury, W. (1981). *Getting to yes: Negotiating agreement without giving in.* Boston, MA: Houghton Mifflin.

Folberg J and Taylor A (1984). Mediation: A comprehensive guide to resolving conflict without litigation. Jossey-Bass: San Francisco.

Framo, J. (1992). *Family of origin therapy: An intergenerational approach.* New York: Routledge.

Framo, J. (2003). *Coming home again: A family-of-origin consultation.* New York: Routledge.

Frankl, V.E. (1956). *The doctor and the soul: From psychotherapy to logotherapy.* New York: Vintage Books.

Freud, S. (1959). *Collected papers.* Jones, E., Ed. New York: Basic Books.

Friedman, E. (1985). *Generation to generation.* New York: Guilford Press.

Friedman, E. (1987, May-June). How to succeed in therapy without really trying. *Family Therapy Networker*, 27–34.

Friedman, E. (1991). Bowen theory and therapy. In A. Gurman & D. Kniskern (Eds.), *Handbook of family therapy, volume 2* (pp. 134–170). New York: Routledge.

Friedman, E. (1996). *Reinventing leadership: Change in an age of anxiety.* New York: Guilford Press.

Friedman, E. (2007). *A failure of nerve: Leadership in the age of the quick fix.* New York: Seabury Books.

Gardner, H. (1983). *Frames of mind.* New York: Basic Books.

Gardner, H. (1993). *Multiple intelligences: The theory in practice.* New York: Basic Books.

Gilbert, R.M. (1996). *A natural systems view of hierarchy.* In P.A. Comella, J. Bader, J.S. Ball, K. Wiseman & R.R. Sagar (Eds.), *The emotional side of organizations: Applications of Bowen theory* (pp. 130–137), Georgetown, MD: Georgetown Family Center.

Gilmore, T. (1982). A *triangular framework: Leadership and followership.* In Sager, R.R. & Wiseman, K.K. (Eds.) *Understanding organizations: Applications of Bowen family systems theory* (pp. 73–94).

Goleman, D. (1994). *Emotional intelligence: Why it can matter more than I.Q.* New York: Bantam Books.

Goleman, D. (2006). *Social Intelligence: The new science of human relationships.* New York: Bantam Books.

Goleman, D., Boyatzis, R. and McKee, A. (2002). *Primal leadership: Realizing the power of emotional intelligence.* Boston, Massachusetts: Harvard Business School Publishing.

Haley, J. (1963). *Strategies of psychotherapy.* New York: Grune & Stratton.

Hilbert, G. (1996). A graduate nursing course using Bowen theory. In P.A. Comella, J. Bader, J.S. Ball, K. Wiseman & R.R. Sagar (Eds.), *The emotional side of organizations: Applications of Bowen theory* (pp. 130–137), Georgetown, MD: Georgetown Family Center.

Kerr, M. (1981). Family systems theory and therapy. In A. Gurman & D. Kniskern (Eds.), *Handbook of family therapy, volume 1* (pp. 226–265). New York: Brunner/ Mazel, Inc.

Kerr, M.E. and Bowen, M. (1988). *Family evaluation: An approach based on Bowen theory.* New York: Norton.

Kichaven, J. (2005, Winter). Mediation advocacy: The state of the art. *Arizona ADR Forum.* Arizona: State Bar of Arizona, ADR Section.

Lederer, W. and Jackson, D. (1968). *The mirages of marriage.* New York: W.W. Norton & Company, Inc.

Lerner, H. (1989). *The dance of intimacy.* New York: Harper Perennial.

MacFarlane, J. & Mayer, B. (2005). What theory? How collaborative problem-solving trainers use theory and research in training and teaching. *Conflict Resolution Quarterly*, 23 (2), 259–276.

MacLean, P. D. (1990). *The triune brain in evolution.* New York: Plenum Press.

Maslow, A.H. (1968). *Toward a psychology of being.* New York: D. Van Nostrand Company.

Mathis, R.D. and Yingling, L.C. (2005). Spousal consensus on the divorce decision and mediation outcome. *Family Court Review*, 29 (1), 56–62.

McCullough, P. (1996). *Leadership from the viewpoint of Bowen theory.* In P.A. Comella, J. Bader, J.S. Ball, K. Wiseman & R.R. Sagar (Eds.), *The emotional side of organizations: Applications of Bowen theory* (pp.130–137), Georgetown, MD: Georgetown Family Center.

McCormick, K. (2009). Personal communication.

Miller, J. (2002). *The anxious organization: Why smart companies do dumb things.* Tempe, AZ: Facts on Demand Press.

Moore, C. (1983). Training in family dispute resolution. *Mediation Quarterly,* 2, 79–89.

Moore, C.W. (1987). The caucus: Private meetings that promote settlement. *Mediation Quarterly,* 16, (87–101).

Moore, C.W. (1996). The mediation process: Practical strategies for resolving conflict. San Francisco, CA: Jossey-Bass.

Mulcahy, L. (2001). The possibilities and desirability of mediator neutrality—Towards an ethic of partiality? Social & Legal Studies, 10 (40), 505–527.

Napier, A. and Whitaker, C. (1978). *The family crucible: The intense experience of family therapy.* New York: Harper & Row Publishers, Inc.

Papero, D.V. (1990). *Bowen family systems theory.* Boston, MA: Allyn and Bacon.

Papp, P. (1994). *The process of change.* New York: Guilford Press.

Raines, S., Hedeen, T., & Barton, A.B. (2010). Best Practices for Mediation Training and Regulation: Preliminary Findings. *Family Law Review,* 48 (3), 551–554.

Regina, W. (2000). Bowen systems theory and mediation. *Mediation Quarterly,* 18 (2), 111–128.

Regina, W. and LeBoy, S. (1991). Incest families: Integrating theory and practice. *Journal of Family Dynamics of Addiction.* 1 (3), 21–30.

Regina, W. and Pace, S. (2008). The personal intelligences in experiential education: A theory in practice. In Warren, K., Mitten, D, & Loeffler, TA (Eds.), *Theory & Practice of Experiential Education,* (pp. 494–506), Boulder, CO: Association for Experiential Education.

Rogers, C. (1951). *Client-centered therapy.* Boston, MA: Houghton Mifflin Company.

Satir, V. (1983). *Conjoint family therapy.* Palo Alto, CA: Science and Behavior Books.

Schnarch, D. (1997). *Passionate marriage: Sex, love and intimacy in emotionally committed relationships.* New York: W.W. Norton & Company, Inc.

Skinner, B.F. (1972). *Beyond freedom and dignity.* New York: Knopf.

Sobel, B. (1982). *Applications of Bowen family systems theory to organizations.* In Sager, R.R. & Wiseman, K.K. (Eds.) *Understanding organizations: Applications of Bowen family systems theory* (pp. 9–22), Georgetown, MD: Georgetown Family Center.

Steinke, P. (2006). *How your church family works: Understanding congregations as emotional systems.* Herndon, VA: Alban Publishing.

Ury, W. (1993). *Getting past no: Negotiating your way from confrontation to cooperation.* New York: Bantam Books.

Whitaker, C.A. & Malone, T.P. (1953). *The roots of psychotherapy.* New York: Blakiston.

Wiseman, K. (1996). Life at work: The view from the bleachers. In P.A. Comella, J. Bader, J.S. Ball, K. Wiseman & R.R. Sagar (Eds.), *The emotional side of organizations: Applications of Bowen theory* (pp. 29–38), Georgetown, MD: Georgetown Family Center.

Wynne, L.C., Ryckoff, I.M., Day, J., & Hirsch, S.I. (1958). Pseudomutuality in the family relationship of schizophrenics. *Psychiatry,* 21, 205–220.

Index

abuse and neglect, 109, 110, 112, 119, 123, 132–34

accusing, 34, 111, 121

acute anxiety, 15, 43, 97. *See also* anxiety

adaptability: and attorneys in mediation, 72; in co-mediation, 71; in differentiating triangles, 63, 64; and differentiation, 13, 14, 61; in domestic mediations, 113; and emotional system, 86; in mediation with stakeholders, 78–80; of mediators, 42; toward immaturity, 80

agreements: Bowen techniques for durable, 84; and caucusing, 91–92; in closing stage, 38; and co-mediation, 55; in developing options stage, 36–37; in differentiating triangles, 64; and differentiation of mediator, 52; in exchange stage, 33; generating multiple options for, 95–98; in mediation with diversity issues, 104; in mediation with stakeholders, 79, 81; mediators' role in facilitating, 40, 42–44; in mediator training, 142, 144; of non-married parents, 117; partial, 38, 119; rejection of, 118–19; and

shuttle mediation, 92–95; writing stage, 37–38. *See also* B SMART agreements; North American model

Agreement to Participate in Mediation form, 28

alcohol, 63, 109–11, 122, 123. *See also* drug addiction

Alternative Dispute Resolution Program, Yavapai County (Arizona) Superior Court, 44. *See also* Yavapai County (Arizona) Superior Court

ambiguity management, 13, 59, 81, 86, 141, 146

amygdala, 25–26, 85, 125, 128–29. *See also* emotional reactivity; limbic system; reptilian brain

anger management, 133

anxiety: in co-mediation, 55; in complicated triangles, 67; differences manifested in, 86; diminishing through clarity, 42; in domestic mediations, 110, 111, 115; and marital conciliations, 122, 123; in mediation, 25–27; in mediation with stakeholders, 79; of mediators, 41, 51, 69; in mediator training, 141, 143, 145, 146; and over- and under-functioning, 46–47; redirection in uninterrupted stage, 31–32; as sign of

CPSIA information can be obtained at www.ICGtesting.com
Printed in the USA
BVOW071143011111

274955BV00003B/1/P